The Wonderful World of Ponies

The Wonderful World of Ponies

Angela Sayer

Hamlyn
London · New York · Sydney · Toronto

Published by The Hamlyn Publishing Group Limited
London · New York · Sydney · Toronto
Astronaut House, Feltham, Middlesex, England

ISBN 0 600 37153 0

Phototypeset by Tradespools Limited, Frome, Somerset
Colour separations by Metric Reproductions, Chelmsford, Essex
Printed in Spain by Mateu Cromo, Madrid

Contents

The evolution and history
of the pony   **6**

Colours and patterns   **15**

Breeds of the world   **22**

Ponies for sport and
pleasure   **45**

Choosing and keeping a
family pony   **65**

Schooling and showing   **84**

Acknowledgements   **96**

The evolution and history of the pony

Above
Przevalsky's Horse is preserved in zoos and parks throughout the world and may be distinguished by its coarse head and mealy muzzle, an upright, dark-striped mane and a sparsely haired tail. The characteristic dun coat has a dark dorsal stripe, and the legs are often marked with zebra stripes.

Right
These small native ponies are grazing in the reedbeds of Lake Awasa in Ethiopa, continuing the centuries-old habits of their forebearers.

In the far off days of the geological period known as the Eocene, the world was a strange, inhospitable place and only the strongest, fittest and most adaptable of species were able to survive. Although great glaciers and ice-fields existed near the poles, much of the Earth enjoyed tropical conditions and succulent flowering trees sprang from the swamplands, undergrown with many forms of flowering plants and shrubs – ideal food and shelter for small browsing mammals. It was in this era that *Eohippus* emerged, the size of a small dog, slight and nervous, its long slender legs finished with splayed feet. With four long toes on each forefoot and three similar toes on each hindfoot, *Eohippus* could run swiftly across the soft marshy ground and thrived on the lush green herbage. As conditions gradually changed over the eons of time, so *Eohippus* also adapted and changed in small, subtle stages and so he came to be known as the 'drawn-horse', for he was the ancestor of all the horses and ponies of the present time.

One of the direct descendants of *Eohippus* was *Miohippus* which arrived in the Miocene period, some twenty million years later. He was larger and more muscular and had one less toe on each fore-

foot. His neck was longer too, enabling his head to reach the newly evolved grasses which were quickly spreading across the plateau lands in which he ranged. Then another twenty million years passed before *Merychippus* emerged, still with three long toes on each foot but now, only the centre toe, longer and enlarged, touched the ground when the animal travelled at speed. In the swamps and marshlands, however, the other toes splayed out, preventing the creature from sinking into the ooze. *Merychippus* was the size of a large dog, and his skull shape was similar to that of today's ponies. His teeth were quite different to those of its forebears being more suited to grinding than to chewing, showing that he was a true grazing, rather than browsing, animal and adapted to life on the open grass plains. His numbers multiplied and the herds spread as the forests dwindled and the prairies grew in size.

Fifteen million years later, *Pliohippus*, some 10 hands high and very fleet of foot, galloped across the plains of the Pliocene period. It was then only one small evolutionary step away from the first true horse, *Equus*, which had real hooves instead of toughened toes and was totally adapted for life as a herd animal of the plains. *Equus* had lost the extra toes and was about 12 hands high and sturdily built. It says much for the nature of his design that almost identical small horses still exist to this very day, namely the Poljakoff or Mongolian Wild Horse (*Equus Przevalskii Przevalskii*). The Poljakoff received its latin name from that of the Russian explorer, Colonel Przevalsky, who discovered a wild herd in 1881 in the Kobdo district of Mongolia. Great excitement was caused by the discovery for it was realized that here were wild horses which had remained virtually unchanged in conformation and appearance since the last Great

Ice Age. Later, in 1902, an expedition went into the Gobi desert to capture some of the horses but because of the difficult terrain and the complete wildness of the animals, it proved impossible to catch any of the adults. Some thirty-two foals were caught, however, which were taken to various zoological parks to establish breeding herds, so that the endangered species could be preserved in captivity.

Luckily the Poljakoff adapted well to its comparatively confined life and proved to be very fertile. The scheme was successful and there are established herds in several countries of the world all safely confined in zoos and parks. In the animal's native land numbers have been severely reduced as a result of hunting, both for game and as food, and it now faces extinction. The Poljakoff is thought to be the ancestor of many breeds of cold-blood horses and ponies, and is a true horse, possessing the strange horny outgrowths, known as chestnuts, on the inside of each leg, a typical horse characteristic. It stands between 12 and 14 hands high and is of varying shades of dun in colour, ranging from the very palest cream-dun through yellow

to the deeper red-dun tones. It has a large coarse head and a stocky, deep-chested body. The points are dark and the muzzle a pale oaten colour. The tail is very sparsely furnished with coarse hair, and the mane forms an upright crest along the neck. Occasionally the legs and haunches may show distinct zebra-like markings, while the spine carries a distinctive dark dorsal stripe.

A dorsal stripe is a breed characteristic of the Tarpan, over which there is great controversy. It was a wild species which flourished in eastern Europe and southern Russia until about 200 years ago when it was learned that the last wild specimen had been hunted down, and shortly afterwards, the remaining horse in captivity had died. And so the Tarpan became officially extinct. It was then that an eminent German zoologist decided to gather together a breeding herd of ponies, all known to be direct descendants of the Tarpan of the steppe lands. He drew up carefully formulated breeding programmes and carried these out under controlled conditions, using the cross-bred stock. Over a period of thirty years, through his genetic expertise, he suc-

Above
Unlike the original Mongolian wild horses, these ponies have flowing manes and tails and neat heads. Their placid attitude as they wait for their riders, indicates that they are also docile and well-mannered.

Right
Despite out-crossing to strengthen the breed this mare shows her descent from the Przevalsky's Horse by the 'zebra marks' on her legs.

Previous page
A modern herd of Mongolian horses moves across the barren Steppes to new grazing, treading in the hoofprints of the ancient herds that lived here, virtually unchanged, since the last great Ice Age.

ceeded in re-creating a herd of Tarpan identical in every way to the original animal which ranged the steppes. That the Tarpan of today is identical to the original animal can be verified by close examination of X-ray photographs of the complete skeleton which resembles the preserved specimens of the eighteenth century in every minute detail.

The Tarpan of today stands about 12 hands high and is of a distinctive mouse-dun colour with a thick black tail and black legs. When living wild in cold regions, herds of Tarpan often grow light coloured, almost white winter coats, as do other species of truly wild animals when subjected to extremely cold and harsh conditions. The Tarpan is, as we shall see later in this book, closely related to many of our present utility ponies and distantly related to most others.

A pony is the term given to any small · variety of horse and is usually taken to mean a horse that is less than 15 hands in height. The height of horses and ponies is measured from the ground, behind the forefoot, up to the top of the bony ridge, known as the withers, where the neck joins the body. A pony is not a young horse, for both horses and ponies give birth to foals; a male foal is known as a colt, while a female foal is a filly. As in horses, the entire male animal is known as a stallion and the female as a mare.

All ponies are of the same basic construction, although obviously some are made for heavy draught work, while others are more elegant and suited only to light riding. They have well-proportioned bodies, powerful hindquarters and shoulders with long, strong necks. The long head has a specially modified jaw and two

sets of teeth. Those in the front of the jaw are used for tearing at grass and herbs which are then passed to the cheek teeth where they are ground into a digestible state before being swallowed. The front teeth undergo distinct and regular changes during the first few years of the pony's life and this enables the expert to accurately determine the animal's age by a brief examination of the pony's dentition.

The pony has small and mobile ears which are usually held in an alert, pricked position. This mobility enables the pony to accurately pinpoint slight unusual sounds which could spell danger. The ears are also useful barometers of a pony's feelings, for when they are held firmly back he is feeling mean and may bite and when they are laid tightly back and flat, he is certain to bite. As in most herbivores the eyes are

large and placed wide apart on either side of the head, giving almost all-round vision. The nostrils are very flexible and are able to flare wide open to pick up the merest scent of an enemy, as well as allowing extra air intake when the animal is galloping in flight. The pony's legs are long for speed and strong for carrying heavy loads. The hooves are of hard, insensitive horn which is constantly renewing itself. The construction of the foot with its wide sole and rubbery frog (the triangular mass in the centre of the sole) helps the pony to be sure-footed over difficult or slippery terrain.

It is thought that ponies migrated from their original homelands of Asia in three main streams, hundreds of years ago. They moved slowly west to Europe, east to China and Mongolia and southwards to India, Persia and Egypt. Small herds settled in areas along the main routes. In their new habitats the ponies diversified and developed through natural selection and were affected by their immediate and differing environments. Colder northern areas produced pony breeds with the ability to grow thick winter coats, while in hotter regions thinner skinned, fine-coated animals came into being. In tropical regions small types of pony evolved, often with very poor conformation but possessing surprising powers of endurance. Later, man intervened in the natural process and by controlling matings, breeds were crossed to produce ponies for special purposes. In this way new breeds were made and then intermated to fix the desirable char-

Above
This is a specimen of the reconstructed breed known as the Tarpan which is identical in every way to the ancient Tarpan, hunted by man to extinction in the eighteenth century.

Above right
Ponies have changed little over the centuries, but manes and tails have become thick and full, and a wide range of coat colours have evolved.

Below right
Innate behaviour patterns have passed unchanged down the generations of the horse family. This little Caspian colt savours subtle scents on the breeze just as his ancestors did thousands of years ago.

acteristics necessary for the work of the particular region. And so over the long generations, each country developed its own native pony breeds.

There is little doubt that man first utilized the pony for food only. At the turn of this century piles of ponies' bones, all split to extract the marrow, were found in a cave in France, the site of prehistoric cavemen dwellings. Other caves are decorated with huge sienna and ochre paintings, some of which depict horses very like the Tarpan, being speared by small human figures. Later, we presume, the smaller ponies would have been tamed to be used as pack animals. As agriculture developed the small, sturdy horse proved invaluable in helping to till the soil and later, with the invention of the collar and refinements in harness, it was used to pull heavier loads.

The first war-horses were quite small ponies and pulled light chariots into battle, and as better ponies were raised, so the chariots were improved until they became instruments of war equipped with blades like the chariot of Boadicea. Eventually man dared to mount the horse, about 3 000 years ago, and from that time the two species have been united in history. Certainly no other species has had the same effect upon the culture of mankind and no other species has so helped man to achieve his aims and ambitions. Having gone into something of a decline with the rapid growth of the technological age, horses and ponies are now experiencing a revived popularity. They are used for all aspects of riding, for pleasure and in competition, for driving and for working the land. In some countries their flesh forms part of the staple diet of the human population, while in other countries this would be considered taboo. People have ponies for many varied reasons, as companions, as status symbols, to ride, drive, jump, to breed from, to love or just for the pleasure of being able to care for them and watch their grace and charm in the paddock. Whatever the reason for having a pony, there is a pony for every purpose, a size to suit every rider and a colour to satisfy everyone's aesthetic taste.

As gene-pools became isolated as, for example, on the Island of Rhum, herds developed distinctive characteristics. The Rhum Ponies are heavily built with flowing manes and tails, and 'feathered' fetlocks.

Colours and patterns

Ponies are found in a wonderful range of colours, certainly one to suit every taste. There are many old superstitions and rhymes concerning the colours and markings, but these have never been proved correct, except perhaps the one that states 'a good horse is never a bad colour'. The order of dominance in the standard colours is grey, bay, brown, black and chestnut. This indicates that grey is dominant to the colours that follow it, then bay is the next most dominant, and so on. From this it is easy to see why so many pony breeds have become predominantly grey in colour, after the introduction of grey stallions to improve type and conformation.

Grey ponies may be of many shades ranging from near white to a dark steel colour. Some have beautiful dappled markings giving the effect of an old-fashioned toy rocking horse, while others are known as 'flea-bitten' because the black hairs present in the white coat are clumped together to form small black dots. Grey ponies are sometimes born almost black and lighten with age. Very old grey ponies may turn pure white. The manes and tails of greys are made of black and white intermingled hairs and the proportions are variable so that one pony may have trimmings which appear pure white while another will look almost black. There are very few pure white ponies and most of these are albino, with very pale eyes and unpigmented skin. Grey ponies are very popular and are extremely attractive when groomed and clean. Many greys have beautiful large dark eyes which further enhance their appearance.

Bay can vary from the colour of polished mahogany to a much paler but rich tone of brown, and bay ponies may be evenly col-

Ponies which appear almost white are called grey, unless they are albino or very old. Greys are always popular and some, like this mare, have large, expressive dark eyes.

Above
Generally considered to be the smartest of all pony colours is the polished mahogany shade known as bay. This placid bay mare has produced an extraordinary foal with clear bay spots on its white coat.

Left
This magnificent stallion is a true bright chestnut colour. Chestnut can vary from a pale reddish-gold to a very dark, distinctive liver-chestnut shade and most ponies of this colour have white markings on their faces and legs.

Right
The palomino is a rich golden shade during the summer, but the winter coat is a pale warm cream. The foals are born cream and take several months to develop their true coat colour.

oured all over, or may have black points. The points are the mane, tail and lower legs. The bay coloration is greatly admired in all equine stock and considered to be very smart in ponies used for showing classes and for driving, unless of course it is a barred colour within a pony's breed standard. Brown can vary from near-bay to a colour which appears to be black and like the bay,

brown ponies often have black points. To distinguish between a dark brown and a black pony it is often necessary to examine the fine short hairs on the muzzle which are a true indication of the animal's colour.

True black ponies are fairly rare, although most of the Fell ponies and similar breeds are black in colour and do well in the show ring. The shiny, short dense

coat of such ponies repays long hours of strapping and grooming by gleaming like satin, reflecting light as the pony trots out before the judges.

Chestnut is a very variable colour and ranges from the very palest red-brown through all the shades of gold to the dark liver-chestnut. Few ponies are completely chestnut, most have striking white marks on their faces and

lower legs which accentuate the glowing coat colour. Some have dark manes and tails, some, like the Haflinger, have white or flaxen trimmings. Chestnuts are generally thought of as being fiery in temperament and rather headstrong, but they are certainly very attractive.

Dun is the colour of the prehistoric ponies, and obviously evolved so that the herds' coloration would merge with that of the dusty plains on which they ranged. Several pony breeds retain this colouring today, often accompanied by the other ancient features of black points and a dorsal or eel line down the back, along the line of the vertebrae. The dun colour is very variable and can be most attractive. The mouse dun is a lilac-grey shade,

the blue-dun is darker, and merely a washed-out black. Golden-dun is a light, warm sandy shade. Dun ponies are considered to be reliable, hard workers, and extremely hardy.

Cream ponies are rare and should have silver manes and tails. They can be of two types, either dominant or recessive genetically, although they may look identical, and only by test-matings can the type be verified. Palomino ponies turn cream in the winter, while their summer coats are the colour of pure gold. They have white manes and tails which must flow freely, untrimmed and unplaited in the show-ring.

The roan effect is caused by intermingling of colours within the pony's coat and is known by

various terms depending upon the proportions of the coloured hairs present. Red, yellow and white hairs merge to give us the strawberry-roan; black, yellow and white hairs make up the blue-roan; chestnut, yellow and white hairs produce the chestnut-roan. Sorrel is very similar to roan, but in this colour only red and black hairs are found, without the white.

Piebald, skewbald and odd-coloured ponies are all known collectively as coloured ponies, and are favoured by the gipsies and horse traders of the world. They were chosen by the Indian tribes of North America in the last century and are still favourites as circus performers in the saw-dust rings of Europe. The pie-bald is generally a white pony

When red and yellow hairs are present in a white coat the effect is called strawberry-roan. Turned out with a grey, this roan has grown fat and well on the summer grass.

Skewbald is the term given to ponies which are white with large irregular brown, bay or chestnut patches. They are great favourites with the North American Indian tribes, possibly because no two ponies are ever identical. Skewbalds are also popular in the circus arena.

with large, irregular patches of black, while the skewbald is white with patches of bay, brown or chestnut. Odd-coloured ponies have patches of two or more colours on the white ground-colour and can be really strikingly marked.

Spotted ponies are very rare and may be marked in several ways – leopard-spotting indicates spots of any colour, clearly defined, on a white or light background. Blanket-spotting occurs when only the rump is white and clearly marked with dark spots. In the snowflake-spotting, the spots are white on a background of any other colour. Spotted horses and ponies have been known for centuries and in Ancient China were known as 'The Heavenly Horses' and considered as sacred animals. They were depicted in Chinese Art from the T'ang Dynasty of a.d. 618–907. Spotted steeds also appear in Egyptian and Greek murals, on the walls of caves in France and on tombs in Italy. Today famous spotted breeds include the Appaloosa, derived from the Palouse country of Idaho, where it was developed by the Nez Percé Indian tribe, and the Danish Knabstrupper breed. Spotted horses and ponies may be of any height and usually have rather thin manes and tails. Many have striped hooves and lots of white around the eyes.

Ponies may be marked in many ways about the head, body and legs and most markings have distinctive terms which must be used in advertisements and for identification purposes. A **star** is the term used to describe any white mark on the pony's forehead, while a **stripe** is a narrow white mark which runs down the face but does not extend beyond the front of the nasal bones. A similar mark which does extend this far is then known as a **blaze**. Any pony with an extensively white head,

where the blaze covers the muzzle or forehead, or is present on the cheeks, is known as **white-faced**. Small, odd white markings, except those on the forehead, are called **snips**. Many ponies have body markings, and a scattering of white hairs is termed **grey-ticked**, black hairs flecked across a light coat are known as **black-marks**, while **zebra-marks** are rare, and show as faint stripes on the neck, withers, quarters and limbs.

Leg markings are usually strikingly white and are often referred to as **socks** or **stockings**. It is more usual to describe the white area more accurately, however, for example **white fetlock** consists of a pale hoof and a white leg to the top of the fetlock joint. There are many old rhymes and superstitions connected with white legs in ponies, one says:

*Four white legs, keep him not a
    day,
Three white legs, send him far
    away.
Two white legs, give him to your
    friend, but
One white leg – keep him to the
    end!*

Out-of-date and unscientific though this may be, many breeders and exhibitors of show-stock seem to prefer one or two white stockings, considering those animals with white 'all round' to be too flashy and unreliable.

Pedigree pony breeds all have carefully formulated standards of points, which set out the requirements for each variety. Such standards include minimum and maximum height restrictions and describe fully the colours or coat patterns allowed within the breed. While owning and showing pedigree ponies can be rewarding, many ponies which are the products of years of cross-breeding can be just as delightful to ride and pet. Such ponies can be of any shape or size or colour. Other ponies, bred especially for riding classes in the show-ring are small versions of the Thoroughbred horse and have all his characteristics suitably scaled down. There is indeed a purpose for every pony, and equally a pony for every purpose.

Above
According to the old rhyme this striking yearling colt should be 'kept not a day' because of his four white legs. His perfect composure at such a tender age, however, disproves such superstition. The white facial marking known as a blaze completes his showy appearance.

Above right
Spotted ponies have been recorded for centuries but are still very rare. Here an Appaloosa mare shares a quiet meadow with two striking blanket-spotted geldings.

Right
Gipsies are fond of strikingly marked ponies whatever their conformation and pay high prices for them. This leopard-spotted colt is kept safely tethered by his neck strap to the back of the caravan.

Breeds of the world

As the islands of the world became populated and human settlements were founded, shipments of livestock often included a few ponies so that these could help with the work of hauling building materials and equipment from the landing beaches to the village site, and clearing and cultivating the land. Naturally, as the years passed, these ponies bred and multiplied and because of the isolating effect of an island habitat, the limited gene-pools caused each herd to become very standardized in shape, size and colour. Even such traits as temperament, tractability and hardiness became fixed after surprisingly few generations. Most islands are proud of their pony herds and care is taken to prevent any undesirable stock mixing with the native ponies.

In 1493, Christopher Columbus landed in Haiti, then called Hispaniola, and put thirty small, tough horses ashore. They had stood up to the three-month voyage from Cadiz, tied on the open deck in the face of rain, wind and storms and with no exercise. It is possible that the present Haiti Pony is a direct descendant of those Spanish imports. The Haiti Pony is certainly tough and hardy and stands about 14 hands high. It may be of any colour, but blacks and browns are the most common. The ponies are used to carry tourists on a difficult four-hour trek to the north of the

Above
Asian ponies are small, tough and wiry and usually ridden and worked in bitless bridles. They are controlled by hardened leather or wooden nosebands with a single, braided rein.

Left
This elegant Sable Island Pony although lightly built is able to withstand extremely harsh conditions on his island home.

Overleaf
This grey pony is being lead by some ingenious headgear as it walks through an enchanting valley near Rabat in Morocco.

island, over rocky terrain, to visit the Citadel Henri Christophe and the Sans-Souci Palace.

Off the Virginian coast of the United States are two small islands, each with their distinctive herds of ponies. Assateague is uninhabited, and the semi-wild ponies are gathered every year to swim across the wide channel to the neighbouring island of Chincoteague. Here the herds of both islands are separately corralled and sorted, then the young stock is put up for auction before the breeding animals are returned to

their territories. About 1 600 kilometres (1 000 miles) northeast of these islands is the uninhabited Sable Island, just off the coast of Nova Scotia. Here small herds of spirited ponies manage to eke out an existence eating the sparse scrub grass which grows through the fine sand. The ponies are descended from New England ponies taken to the island early in the eighteenth century when there was a small settlement there. Although the island is inhospitable with no trees or shelter of any kind, and

suffers extreme winter cold, the Sable Island Pony is lightly built and elegant, about 14 hands high and often dark chestnut in colour.

Of the 3 000 islands which make up Indonesia, many are totally dependent on their ponies for all forms of transport, sport and pleasure. Many of the islands are devoid of roads and have very poor grazing, so the ponies have to be hardy and tireless as well as versatile. The most elegant and best-bred pony in Indonesia is the Sandalwood, so called because the two main exports of the island

of Sumba where they are found, are the ponies and the rare sandalwood timber. The Sandalwood stands about 13 hands high and has an Arabian-type head, hard, clean joints and a fine silky coat, unlike that of other Indonesian pony breeds. The finest ponies of the breed are used for spring racing over 5 000-metre (16 000-feet) distance and are ridden without saddles or bits, but wearing a plaited leather bridle with a hardened noseband, identical to those used in Central Asia, 4 000 years ago. Sandalwood ponies are intelligent and strong, and rarely sweat up even after racing.

Also on Sumba, and the neighbouring Sumbawa, are found ponies with the same names. The Sumba Pony is of an ancient type, usually dun in colour with dark points and a dorsal stripe. Intelligent and willing, many are taught to dance by their owners, who fit bells to their animals' forelegs and compete with other owners in competitions. The ponies are held on lunge-reins, usually with a small child riding bareback, and dance to the beat of skin-covered drums. The Sumbawa Pony is similar to the Sumba and very docile. It is always ridden and worked in a bitless bridle and

often used in mounted games, in which lances are thrown at opponents while riding at full gallop.

The Timor Island Pony is small, usually under 12 hands, but is very robust and agile and carries an adult man with no difficulty over rough ground. The Java Island Pony is a little larger and stronger and, although his conformation is poor, is an excellent draught animal, and is used for drawing 'sados' (two-wheeled carts), which are piled high with produce and people. On Sumatra is found the Batak Pony; the mares of this breed are sent to Arabian stallions to constantly improve the stock. The Indonesian government control the breeding and sale of the Batak progeny, sending it to other islands to strengthen the breeding herds. The Bali Pony is about 13 hands high and very similar to the Poljakoff – dun with black dorsal stripe and occasionally exhibiting an upright mane. Bali Ponies are used for riding and as pack ponies, carrying heavy panniers of stones from the island shores for building walls and tracks.

Iceland Ponies arrived with early settlers from Norway in the ninth century and, later, ponies

Above
In contrast this striking bay, showing traces of Oriental bloodlines, is bridled with thick leather and chain. The bit has been removed so that he may graze more comfortably as he rests, in the Turkish Alps.

Right
This small, stocky pony is used in Iceland for draught purposes. Such ponies are intelligent and have a strongly developed homing instinct; their thick coats protect them from the extreme climate.

were imported from Ireland. The early settlers indulged in the sport of horse-fighting, and so needed strong, spirited animals. Until the islanders were converted to Christianity in the tenth century, their ponies also formed part of their staple diet. Nowadays, two distinct types of Iceland Pony may be found: one used generally for draught work, while the finer type is used mainly for riding. The draught ponies are short and stocky and extremely hardy, while the riding ponies are lighter, with finer bone. Both types share the same intelligence and the almost uncanny homing instinct, present in all horses, but much more pronounced in the Iceland breed.

The riding ponies are trained to perform an ambling trot known as the tølt which is comfortable for the rider and covers the rough ground economically. They are controlled mainly by the voice, and though as independent as most small ponies, are charming and friendly.

The Faroe Islands lie 400 kilometres (250 miles) south-east off Iceland and have ponies of a very similar type and conformation, stemming from the same stock. The Faroe Island Pony is usually dark brown or chestnut, with the occasional black, while the Icelander is nearly always grey, sometimes dun and only rarely brown, or chestnut.

The British Isles are rich in pony breeds. Scotland has two breeds, the Highland and the Shetland, England has five breeds, the Exmoor, Dartmoor, Dales, Fell and New Forest, while Wales has its famous Mountain Pony and Ireland the Connemara. The climate and geology is ideal for raising ponies which are used for all manner of purposes, and exported to all corners of the Earth.

The Exmoor Pony is perhaps the most ancient of the British breeds, and has certainly roamed the Exmoor area for centuries. It is thought to be a direct descendant of the native British wild horse and so can be described as an

indigenous breed, although the first horses must have crossed the landbridge to Britain when it was still joined to the rest of Europe. Finely built and 12·2 hands high the Exmoor, with its characteristic 'mealy' nose and rich, dark colouring, is a strong little pony and capable of carrying a man at speed across the moors for hours. Ponies of this breed make ideal mounts for small children, being narrow and sure-footed; they also go well in harness.

Dartmoor, in England's extreme south-west is grim and forbidding, but its rocky slopes and boggy gullies are home to another hardy pony breed. Unlike the Exmoor which has remained virtually pure-bred through the centuries, the Dartmoor has had infusions of other blood, for Thoroughbred, Arabian, Hackney and other native breed stallions have all run on the moor from time to time. In more recent times stricter control has been exercised and the true Dartmoor Pony has been standardized. It should be bay, black or brown

with a small, well-bred head, small alert ears, strong shoulders and back. The tail must be set high and the feet must be tough and well-shaped. The ponies are allowed to breed naturally on the moor, but the best stock is kept safely in private studs, being brought out for an annual sale at Exeter each year.

In the New Forest in the south of England, some 3 000 ponies roam, exercising the rights of the people to graze their stock on the 'common' land. Although there are few boundaries to control the ponies in the 17 800 hectares (43 000 acres), it has been found that the animals have distinct grazing territories and do not roam outside these. New Forest ponies are branded or marked in other ways, and an annual round-up is conducted in the autumn when young stock is caught and identified along with the older animals. A sale follows and unwanted animals are disposed of, often going as riding ponies for which their even temperament makes them ideal. The New

Forest Pony is fairly large, up to 14 hands in height and may be of any colour. This size and strength, combined with its friendliness and care in crossing rough country make this breed ideal as a general-purpose family pony.

The north of England is the natural home of two large, heavy breeds of pony which both stem from the same roots, but developed on opposite sides of the Pennine Mountain Ridge, and so formed two distinct breeds. On the east of the ridge came the magnificent Dales Pony, while on the west side the Fell Pony was developed. The Dales Pony can be up to 14·2 hands high and is usually black, bay or dark brown. It is an exceptionally strong pony with a true pony head, short strong neck, straight shoulders and a muscular back. The tail is set rather low and the fetlocks have the long fine hairs known as 'feathers'. Ponies of this breed are ideal for riding and are strong enough to carry the heaviest adult. They are used extensively for driving and in agriculture, and are also economical to keep. Dales have a good straight action at all paces, and some famous examples of the breed have set up records for endurance trotting.

It is thought that the Romans brought some heavy Friesian horses to Britain when they found the indigenous breeds too small to haul the stonework for their fortifications, and later the imported stock crossed with the native mares and so produced the ancestors of the Dales and Fells. The Fell Pony is generally smaller than its cousin and is most commonly black although brown is sometimes seen and the occasional bay. Although it was formally a pack pony, the Fell is an ideal riding pony, being surefooted, strong and with a comfortable action. This breed is carefully preserved and kept pure, and is easily recognized with its abundant, waved black mane and tail and feathered heels.

The Welsh Mountain Pony has a recorded and verified history which goes back to the days of Julius Caesar who bred ponies under controlled conditions on the shores of Lake Bala in Wales. This breed is confusing to the novice for it is registered in four sections and numbered A, B, C and D. The Welsh Mountain Pony Section A is the smallest and obviously the original breed from which the other section types have sprung. It must not measure more than 12 hands in

Above
New Forest Ponies are fairly large and can be of almost any colour. Being good-natured and very sure-footed, they make excellent family ponies.

Above right
The Fell Pony is a heavy breed used originally for draught and pack work, but has now been pressed into service as a family pony. Gentle enough to be ridden by a small child, the Fell is also strong enough to carry a heavy man.

Below right
This exquisite little Mountain Pony mare shows the influence of her Arabian forebears in her fine bone and elegant head as she grazes quietly with her young foal.

The Welsh Ponies and Cobs form a fascinating group among the British native pony breeds. There are four distinct types, each with its own characteristics and section in the official stud-book.

Above left
The Welsh Mountain Pony, under
12.2 hands, is classed in Section A.
This is a bay colt of great promise
and shows the classically beautiful
conformation of the type.

Left
This grey stallion is a fine Welsh
Pony, Section B, similar in build to
the Section A but up to 13.2 hands
in height.

Above right
This is a Welsh Cob, Section D; he is
a two-year-old colt with a rare
chestnut-roan colour, and still
immature in build. Sections C and D
have the same basic standards for
type, but Section C animals measure
up to 13.2 hands while Section D may
be as large as 15.2 hands, as long as
they retain their pony characteristics.

Right
This is a magnificent black stallion of
excellent conformation. He is a Welsh
Pony of Cob type, Section C, and is
strong and muscular.

height, but is strong and hardy with a delicate small head. It makes an ideal first pony for children learning to ride and can prove to be an exceptionally good jumper. Usually grey, brown or chestnut, other colours are allowed except piebald and skewbald. The Section B Pony is a riding pony of character and may be up to 13·2 hands and is one of the world's most popular breeds, having been exported to many countries. The Section C is known as the Welsh Pony of Cob Type which is also up to a height of 13·2 hands, while the Section D is the genuine Welsh Cob which is allowed to be as large as 15·2 hands high but must retain its true pony type.

It is easy to see how the four types came into being. First of all the original Mountain Ponies were loved for their vigour and good, willing temperament. They are the fairies among native ponies with their delightful 'look of eagles' inherited from the Arabian stock infused by the Romans. As the standards called for the height restriction of 12 hands, ponies which grew above this size had to be discarded from

Above
The diminutive Shetland Pony, which was originally used for transporting seaweed, for use as fertilizer, has become one of the best known of all the world's pony breeds. Shetlands breed best in natural conditions, each stallion running with a small herd of mares and their tiny, woolly-coated foals.

Right
Connemara Ponies are loved by all who take the trouble to get to know them. Friendly and versatile, they make excellent family ponies and usually jump well.

future breeding programmes. Some of these 'rejects' were perfect, except that they were too large and so the Welsh Pony was born, and proved to be a success for general purposes and in the show ring, especially as a jumper. The tiny Mountain Pony and the Welsh Cob, when crossed produced an all-purpose pony, fine enough to ride and strong enough to drive, as well as being the perfect mount for the inexperienced rider to take on a trek through the beautiful mountains of Wales. The strongest and perhaps most useful of the four sections is the Welsh Cob which can carry a rider of any weight and does all a horse can do without needing so much food or special attention. In harness, the Welsh Cob looks particularly well and has an exaggerated, showy action at the trot.

Two types of pony were bred in Scotland: the Mainland, and the Western Isles, and although it was the latter which was the oldest and purest of the two types, it is the Mainland which is now known as the Highland Pony. Surely the most versatile of all the British native ponies, the Highland has recently enjoyed a well deserved surge of popularity. Highlands vary in height between 13 and 14.2 hands and are strong and well made while retaining true pony type. They have long been regarded as utility animals and for generations served as pack ponies quite capable of carrying great weights, such as the carcases of Red Deer, down the steep and treacherous mountain paths.

The breed makes an excellent family pony, being strong enough to carry the adults and gentle enough to be trusted with young

children. Highland Ponies are exceptionally good in the hunting field where their intelligent appraisal of any situation stands them in good stead. Perhaps the most interesting feature of the Highland Pony is the great range of colours in which it may be found, for in addition to the usual grey, brown and black there are beautiful bays and deep liver-chestnuts sporting silver manes and tails. Many original Highlands were of the primitive yellow dun colour with black points, but many variations of duns are now seen from the silvery mouse-dun through cream, silver and gold. With long and flowing, waved manes and tails the benign Highland is a beautiful pony.

By far the smallest of the British ponies is the diminutive Shet-land, which is a native of the most northern of the British Isles, Orkney and Shetland. Its small size was produced by years of existing under harsh conditions in an inhospitable environment. When food is scarce and shelter limited a small animal is at an advantage for it needs less to eat and has less body area from which to lose heat than a larger animal. What it lacks in size the Shetland makes up for in personality and it can be a clown among ponies. Indeed many Shetlands grace the circus rings of the world and perform their tricks and paces with dignity and precision. Although too tiny for all but the smallest riders, Shetlands go well in harness and for their size are among the strongest of all breeds. Shetlands were exported to America where they have developed as a separate and distinct breed rather like miniature Hackney ponies. They are shown in harness and renowned for their high, exaggerated action and are often fitted with long false hooves and flowing false tails.

On the west side of Ireland is the windswept region known as the Connemara in which evolved a beautiful breed of native pony, between 13 and 14 hands high and with an elegant conformation. Most commonly found in various shades of grey, however black, brown, bay and dun also occur and until recently, dun ponies with black dorsal stripes were common in the area. The development of the Connemara as a breed was established, without interference from man, by the

Left
A herd of Lundy Island Ponies sip fresh rainwater from a pool on the island's high granite plateau. Strong and wiry enough to withstand the harsh winter conditions, they are also extremely agile and make wonderful jumping ponies for young children.

Right
A lone grey Camargue Pony forages among the reed beds in the marshlands of the Rhône valley.

Below
These sturdy chestnut Haflinger Ponies with their distinctively light manes and tails, seem unperturbed by the harsh weather. Protected by dense winter coats, they herd patiently together while waiting for their hay rations.

geography of the area. The climate of the Connemara region is similar to that of Southern Europe and lush herbage is available for grazing from very early spring until late in the year. The soil is enriched with minerals which contribute greatly to the strength and quality of the ponies' bone. In the nineteenth century some Arabian and Welsh crosses were made in the Connemara herds and the Arabian influence is evident in the beautiful heads of today's ponies. Pure-bred and part-bred Connemara ponies are renowned for their excellence in all spheres of riding activity and are in great demand in many countries of the world.

Connemara and Exmoor stallions have been used in the establishment of a fine breeding herd of ponies on the granite island of Lundy, forty kilometres (twenty-five miles) off the Devonshire coast. Home of Gannets, Puffins and other large seabirds, Lundy Island is a flat, grassy and windswept plateau about five kilometres (three miles) long and 0·8 kilometres (half a mile) wide, from which steep, spectacular granite cliffs slide into the sea. Lundy Island Ponies are dun in colour and stand about 13·2 hands high. They are very hardy products of their environment, but full of quality and substance. In 1929 a batch of forty-two New Forest mares was taken to the island by ship and breeding plans were formulated. Over the years a distinct type has emerged due to the rigid selection of dedicated islanders, and the Lundy Pony is now established as a distinctive and admirable variety.

Also a genuine product of its environment is the Camargue Pony which lives in herds in a semi-wild state in the salt marshes around the mouth of the river Rhône. Obviously descended from Oriental stock these ponies are used for herding the wild black Camargue bulls, which breed alongside them on the marshlands and are much prized for their arrogance and pride in the bull-ring. The Camargue ponies are well made about 14·2 hands high. They are usually grey in colour and range from near white to a dark blue-grey, with foals born dark grey, almost black, turning paler as they grow. These ponies suffer great hardship being ridden hard by the local cowboys and existing on very poor grazing, often up to their bellies in salt water as they forage for herbage among the reed beds. In summer they are used to carry tourists through the treacherous marshes to view the great flocks of pink flamingoes that inhabit the region, while in winter they are turned loose to fend for themselves. When the herds gallop through the marsh waters with only their heads and shoulders visible in the spray they resemble the proverbial 'wild white horses of the sea', a name by which they are sometimes known.

In Germany there are two native pony breeds, the hardy but almost extinct Senner Pony which roams the Teutoburger Wald, south of Osnabruck, and the Dülmen which lives semi-wild in Meerfelder Bruch. The Dülmen has lived in the region for at least six centuries and the herds are gathered up annually so that unwanted stock can be sold. Less than 13 hands in height, Dülmen Ponies may be of any colour though brown, black and dun predominate, the dun showing black points and a dorsal stripe.

The dorsal stripe, an indication of direct descent from the Tarpan, is also exhibited by some of

the Polish pony breeds. The nearest domesticated relative of the Tarpan is obviously the Konik, 13 hands and very compact, which is found in all shades of yellow-, grey- or blue-dun. Its smaller cousin is the Huzul, a hardy tireless mountain breed which is sometimes known as the Carpathian Pony. Both these ponies are of ancient origin and it is good to know that they are being carefully preserved.

An ideal mountain pony and one that is in great demand in many countries wherever a small, sturdy pack-pony is needed is the Austrian Haflinger. Often described as being a 'prince in front and a peasant behind' this pony is like a small golden horse. The Haflinger is bright chestnut and usually has a flaxen or white mane and tail. About 14 hands high and strong, with an easy flowing stride, this pony is equally useful for riding or draughtwork, and has a happy, outgoing nature. In Italy, the Avelignese is similarly descended, but slightly larger and heavier than the Haflinger.

Sweden's native pony is another island pony; the direct descendant of an ancient breed,

for many years it bred undisturbed on the island of Gotland. A century ago two stallions were introduced to improve the stock, one a Syrian horse and the other an Oriental stallion, but the type was well fixed and remains unchanged. Skeletons of ancient Gotland Ponies have been excavated in caves on the island and date back to the Stone Age. They bear a close resemblance to the Gotland Pony of today. These well-made ponies of about 12 hands high come in several colours and are in great demand as riding ponies for young children, farmers' utility ponies, and for pony trotting races.

The endearing Fjord or Westlands Pony of Norway looks as though it had trotted straight out of the Ice Age, for it bears a striking resemblance to its ancestors, the wild horses of Mongolia. It is either cream- or yellow-dun with a dark mane and tail and the distinctive dorsal stripe; stripes on the legs are also occasionally seen. Unchanged since it carried the Vikings to victory in their hand-to-hand horse-fighting contests, the Fjord is strong and sturdy, alert and active, with a grand

sense of humour. Equally good for riding or in harness this breed is in great demand in many north European countries where it is ideal for working the light agricultural soils.

Norway's Northlands Pony is a very rare breed directly descended from the Tarpan. This is a small, dark-coloured pony with a very full and flowing mane and tail and is said to closely resemble the now extinct Lofoten Island Pony. The Döle-Gudbrandsdal is much larger and closely resembles the British Fell Pony. This pony was produced by mixing Danish heavy horses with some Thoroughbred and Trotter stallions, and this has produced a pony which can pull a heavy load at a smart trotting pace for long distances.

The Greek Islands were once rich in pony breeds but these have gradually died out over the years although there are a few quite distinctive ponies to be found. The Peneia Pony is of Oriental type and varies considerably in height and colour. It is used for pack-work and in agriculture and has been found to be very economical to feed. Stal-

lions of this breed are often put to donkey mares, producing excellent hinnies.

In the mountains of Thessaly the Pindos Pony is used for riding and farm work. It is very similar to the Peneia Pony and decidedly Oriental in type. These ponies are very sure-footed and invaluable for traversing the hilly slopes of the region, often heavily weighted down with produce for market. The Island of Skyros supports 11-hand ponies of the Tarpan type, of poor conformation due, probably, to the sparse grazing available. These ponies are usually dun, grey or brown and are exported from the island as first riding ponies for very small children. On the island the ponies are used in teams to thresh corn and for carrying water. These tiny ponies were in danger of dying out in recent years but luckily a society was formed which sent aid in the form of food and veterinary treatment, and is working for the breed's preservation.

The delightful Caspian is a breed of pony which was thought to be extinct. This pony looks and moves like a miniature Arabian horse, indeed it has been suggested that it may well have been the ancestor of the Arabian of

Left
Famous for its endurance and pulling power, the Döle-Gudbrandsdal is used extensively on farms and small-holdings in Norway.

Above
In the Greek Islands ponies are still used in agriculture. This little chestnut is trotting in decreasing circles over cut wheat, threshing the seed from the husks.

Mehran, a famous Caspian Pony stallion foaled in Iran, now grazes in safe English pastures surrounded by his mares.

today. The rediscovery of the Caspian Pony is a modern fairytale; in 1965 an expedition was sent to the shores of the Caspian Sea in North Iran to discover if there were any small ponies in the region suitable for teaching small children to ride. Dedicated horse-lovers were delighted to learn that perfectly formed miniature horses had been found and steps were taken to extract sufficient numbers of breeding mares and stallions to ensure the breed's survival. The Caspians were purchased from between the shafts of laden carts, and taken from under back-breaking loads of faggots; they were discovered high in the mountains and in the mud of the rice paddies. Some were sick, some were bruised and had been sorely treated, all were riddled with parasites. Slowly the breeding stock was selected by picking the very best of the ponies as foundation animals.

A stud was established just outside Tehran where the ponies were treated and carefully studied as well as being bred from; studs of breeding stock have also been started in Britain, Bermuda and the United States. The Caspian is a beautiful pony with a short, fine head, large dark eyes and low, flaring nostrils. The ears are very short and alert. The slim graceful neck leads into good withers and sloping shoulders, the back is straight, the body slim and the tail set high. The slim legs have dense bone and the fetlocks are clean of all feathering. The hooves are particularly noticeable, being extremely hard and strong and oval in shape. In temperament the Caspians are intelligent and willing, and even stallions at stud may be worked together or put in the same paddock. At all paces this pony is smooth and comfortable and it has an amazing ability for jumping. In fact the Caspian Pony is a miniature horse which has galloped from the pages of the past into the present day.

Ponies for sport and pleasure

Polo is a very ancient game, a form of which was played in Persia as long ago as 500 b.c. Ancient manuscripts bear illuminations showing colourfully garbed riders, on spirited ponies, wielding sticks which look very similar to those used today. The game in which the eager participants are involved is clearly a form of polo and is thought to have evolved from another, more dangerous mounted game called Savlajam, in which a solid ball was knocked high in the air. In Isfahan may be found the ruins of an ancient polo ground some 300 metres (984 feet) long and with stone goalposts still standing firm at either end. The beautiful pavilion from which the Shah Abbas used to watch the matches still exists, but instead of pounding hooves the central arena is now trod only by the feet of sightseers and tourists who may wander among the flower beds and around the central pool which now adorns the space. The sport was popular in Persia for centuries; a match between Persian and Turkish riders was described in an exciting poem by the Persian poet Firdawi in a.d. 935.

From Persia the game spread far and wide and in the Himalayas there is a natural rocky amphitheatre where the sport has been practised for over 2 000 years. At the entrance may be found a rough wooden sign which reads, in English: 'Let other men do other things – The King of Sports is still the Sport of Kings.' In the more northerly Pamir range of mountains, in Russia, the game is played on tough wiry ponies, and is called 'guibosi'. Throughout the countries of Tibet, India, China and Japan the sport of polo, or similar games, became popular wherever the local nimble ponies could produce an adequate turn of speed.

In this picture the pony nearest the camera is trying to ride-off the other pony to prevent its rider from hitting the ball.

In polo, said to be the King of Sports, two teams of four players compete against each other in periods of play known as chukkers. Each game usually consists of four to six chukkers.

alterations, one being the restriction to a height limit for ponies, they have changed very little in the last 100 years. Twenty years later in the 1880s, polo became popular in the United States, then rapidly spread to South America until today there are very few places in the world where polo is not played.

Just as polo may be said to be the King of Sports, the polo pony can be said to be the King of Ponies. A Polo Pony can be of any colour and its characteristics vary according to the country of its birth. Several breeds have been used to develop suitable animals for this exacting game and the most successful ponies have strong, short backs, long necks and very muscular quarters. Above all the Polo Pony must be extra intelligent and have a natural aptitude for the game. It must be obedient and responsive at all paces, and from an early age it is trained to perform lightning starts and stops and to turn on pressure from the reins across the neck and the weight of the rider's body, rather than on direction on the bit. Ponies bred in Argentina are especially sought after by top polo riders, for they are exceptionally fast and quite fearless. These ponies have been crossed with Thoroughbreds and with ponies from India and Pakistan as well as Connemara and New Forest Ponies. Over the years a fairly standard type known as the Polo Pony has emerged.

Although most equines used for racing are full-sized horses, some countries do enjoy pony racing as a sport and the animals are raced on the flat in the normal way, or drawing small vehicles in trotting races. Trotting races are very popular in many European countries where famous studs breed specialized ponies as Trotters. In France the Noram Trotter is from Thoroughbred stock and is usually horse-sized, although one famous Italian-bred Noram which won 129 races was only 14 hands high, and ponysized. In Holland trotting has been a national sport for some years and the breed of Trotter known as the Harddraver has been developed. This breed was very successful and some stock was exported to the United States to help found the American Trotter there. The circle was com-

British cavalry officers first watched, then learned to participate in the game of polo, while serving overseas, and it was eventually introduced to Britain in 1859. When the officers of the 10th Hussars returned from the North West Frontier of India in 1871, the game became well established and four years later a governing body, the Hurlingham Polo Association, was formed. This body drew up exacting rules to be followed in playing the game, and apart from minor

pleted when American Trotters reached their peak, and breeding stock was exported to European countries to improve all racing Trotter stock.

Italy has the greatest trotting race fans in the world, and Palermo in Sicily has a wonderful track where the crowds throng to cheer their favourites home. In Russia, competitive trotting races have been popular for many years and their own breed, the Orlov Trotter, was established in 1778 from Thoroughbred, Arabian and Harddraver stallions and mares. The Orlov Trotter had to perform equally well in a racing sulky on hard ground or drawing a sleigh over a snow-packed track. Eventually, with the importation of American Trotter stock, an even harder and faster strain was raised and became known as the Russian Trotter. Animals of this line are used for agriculture and in transportation as well as for racing. The Scandinavian countries all indulge in Trotting races, Norway with the Döle Trotter,

Trotting races are popular in many countries of the world. The ponies draw specially constructed lightweight wheeled vehicles called sulkies and must trot-out for the duration of the race without breaking step into a canter or gallop.

Sweden with the North Swedish Trotter and Finland with the Finnish Universal. Canada, Australia and New Zealand have also made trotting races a popular leisure pastime and great crowds support the meetings, chancing their wages on the ponies they fancy.

Ponies used for show-jumping can be of any colour, breed or conformation. Their only attribute must be the ability to jump accurately and safely, carrying their rider over all manner of high, wide and difficult obstacles. In show-jumping, ponies are subject to height restrictions, juvenile ponies, for instance, must not exceed 14.2 hands high, but a 12.7mm (half-inch) allowance is made for their shoes. A pony with natural aptitude and the right breeding and conformation for jumping must be carefully schooled to instil the right degree of suppleness and obedience. Eventually its ability can be assessed and its potential as a jumper accurately determined. Some ponies jump slowly but can attain surprising heights, others jump neatly and economically at speed and so are excellent for competitions timed 'against the clock'. Some ponies jump best when performing in indoor arenas while others only do well in the open. Quite often a heavier pony with its very muscular quarters proves to be an outstanding jumper though quite unsuitable for any other aspects of showing.

For hunting, a sport carried on in most countries where horse-riding is popular, it is usual to ride a Hunter or other similar horse, but as horse-keeping becomes more and more expensive, so an increasing number of people are turning to the smaller breeds as mounts. Of all these the Welsh Cob proves to be ideal. As we have seen in chapter three, the Welsh Pony can be of Cob type, up to a height of 13.2 hands, and the Welsh Cob Section D which can be larger. The Cob has the stride and ride of a horse combined with the intelligence, liveliness and economy of a pony. The type for Section C and Section D animals is the same and calls for a fine pony head complete with large and intelligent eyes. The Cob must have good bone, strong hocks, good feet and an even, kind temperament.

Above left
Some ponies are trained to run in a manner known as pacing. In this the legs on the same side go forward simultaneously, quite unlike the motion of the trot. Pacing is very fast and the ponies must not break stride. To ensure that the legs move in the prescribed manner a special harness is suspended around the animals' limbs.

Left
This pony is obviously a safe and accurate jumper and his rider assists him by maintaining an excellent forward seat and good contact with the reins as he clears the rails.

Above
The thrill of the chase encourages even the smallest pony to jump formidable obstacles.

Right
This rider should refrain from allowing his pony to graze on a loose rein while waiting at the covert. In an emergency he would have no control over his mount.

The Welsh Cob is game for any event and has sufficient stamina to carry an adult all day in the hunting field. He is possessed of a natural, safe jumping ability and gives the impression of always enjoying its work. If the cob is kept out at grass all year he will obviously need extra rations for the strenuous hunting season and will need clipping out when his winter coat has grown, although the legs must be left. A New Zealand rug, maintained in good condition and properly fitted will then keep him snugly warm whatever the weather. A pony kept in this way needs only a light groom-ing before being tacked-up and taken to the meet on the morning of the hunt. On his return at the end of the day he must be allowed to cool off completely, be watered, then fed before the New Zealand is replaced and he is turned out to relax.

Other heavier breeds of pony also make ideal hunters, especially if they have been encouraged to develop their natural jumping ability. The Fells, Dales and Connemaras all give good ac-counts of themselves when fol-lowing hounds and do not 'hot-up' and misbehave like some of the smaller breeds. Often these

Shetland Ponies go well in harness and are generally quiet enough to be driven by quite small children in the confines of a garden or park.

are trace clipped, that is clipped in a straight line along the body and all the hair beneath this line is removed except on the legs. The pony is then able to keep cooler during a hard day's work than if he was carrying a full coat. Ponies really seem to enjoy a day with hounds and, unless they are fed too much corn, behave themselves in a composed manner. It is important for young ponies to learn their manners by attending one or two meets in order to get the feel of the occasion before staying out all day. This way they become accustomed to being in

the close proximity of lots of other horses and ponies and the pack of hounds. Any tendency to kick should be firmly discouraged, and over-excitement should be curbed.

Driving is a growing sport. More and more societies are formed each year and ponies of every breed and type are harnessed to every conceivable form of wheeled vehicle. There are driving meets, driving marathons, harness parades, obstacle races, scurry races and every kind of event imaginable. Ponies are driven singly, in pairs, and as a

tandem or a team. They must be well-made and strong as well as being carefully broken to harness. Their manners in traffic must, of course, be impeccable and they must start and stop without hesitation. The Hackney Pony has been bred for over 200 years and is descended from the Thoroughbred and the Norfolk Trotter crossed with British native ponies. It is a very showy pony with a high action. Years ago the Hackney was expected to trot at least 27·3 kilometres (seventeen miles) in one hour. A pair or tandem of Hackney ponies is a magnificent

sight to behold as the turnout spanks smartly around a show ring. Bred originally in Britain, the Hackney Pony can be found in every country where driving is a popular sport.

Perhaps the most popular sport of all for the pony is the gymkhana. Every pony can have a try at one or other of the many and varied events that are offered, and great fun is had by all, the ponies, the riders and the spectators. This is one mounted sport where the small pony can often beat the larger one, for most gymkhana games depend upon the skill and

In Ireland, local ponies pull special carts with seats that face outwards, to carry tourists on pleasant trips around the green countryside. These vehicles are called jaunting carts and are kept, like the ponies, in excellent condition.

agility of the pony in response to its rider's aids. Some ponies learn to play all the gymkhana games and seem to thoroughly enjoy them, turning, stopping and riding off other ponies without really waiting for their rider's signals.

Participation in mounted games develops in the rider an unconscious sense of balance and a good seat, and in the pony it encourages extra use of the hocks and haunches, and generally improves his handiness. In training a pony for gymkhana events or mounted games, basic schooling comes first and he must walk, trot and canter, changing pace immediately the aids are applied. He must go forward eagerly when signalled to do so and must stop promptly from any pace. It is important that the gymkhana pony is taught to stand while being mounted, even in the excited

atmosphere of a crowded ring, with other ponies rushing in different directions. This is difficult to achieve for it is the pony's most natural instinct to run with the herd. He must also learn to be unafraid of such strange sights as his rider hopping along half encased in a bran-sack, or frantically attempting to bite an apple from a swinging string. The pony must learn to run next to his rider on a loose rein and not to pull back; to allow his rider to carry strange equipment such as a straw-filled dummy, a bucket, an umbrella or a precariously balanced egg on a wooden spoon. Above all the rider must learn to perform these exhilarating games without allowing the excitement to overcome good riding techniques. All too often the spectators are treated to an upsetting display of flapping arms and legs, ponies being shouted at and yanked in

the mouth by inconsiderate riders. Luckily it is the well-schooled and disciplined pony with a sympathetic and practised rider that wins the events, so the losers learn by example.

Rodeo riding can only be described as a spectator sport within the pages of this book, for it is a dangerous pursuit, very popular in the United States of America. Among other events, experienced cowboys try their luck at riding strong ponies renowned for their ability to buck, and known as bronchos. Most of the riders are professionals who travel the rodeo circuit, thrilling the crowds with their skill and nerve. The broncho-riding events are in two classes, saddled and bareback, and the cowboys draw lots to see which ponies they will have to ride. Some bronchos are much more difficult than the others, and some learn to buck in a very lethal

Left
In colder countries, pairs of ponies draw sleighs over the hard-packed snow and are usually fitted with special shoes to enable them to keep their feet in the slippery conditions.

Right
Hackney Ponies are renowned for their distinctive high-stepping action. With its proud bearing this fine black draws applause from the crowd as it trots smartly around the show-ring.

Below right
Ponies seem to enjoy the thrill of competing as much as their young riders when the event is as exciting as a gymkhana bending race.

Overleaf
This quietly grazing mare and her piebald foal are well-away from all the bustle of shows and gymkhanas.

manner. The word broncho is derived from a Spanish term meaning 'rough and rude' and is very apt for these wild and wilful animals.

The bronchos are put into specially constructed chutes with high, narrow wooden sides which prevent them from turning around. If the event is for saddled riding, the saddles are lowered on to the bronchos from above, and the rider tightens the girth through the side of the barricade. Often the pony will start to buck within the confines of the chute. When the arena is cleared the first rider lowers himself into the saddle of his alloted mount and takes a firm hold on the single rope attached to the pony's head collar and signals that he is ready. The chute door is released and springs wide open, the broncho bounds out in a cloud of dust head down and bucking furiously to

This hardy grey pony flying for the finish of the egg-and-spoon race will unfortunately be disqualified as the rider appears to have dropped her egg.

unseat the rider. The cowboy has to obey certain rules of riding to score high points. His free arm must swing to and fro level with his shoulder and only one hand must grip the rope. He must not grasp the broncho's mane or grip its sides with his legs. His spurred boots must brush the bucking pony's sides from shoulder to flank continuously throughout the ride to show that he is remaining in the saddle by skilful balance alone. Quite often the cowboy is knocked slightly off balance by the very first leaping buck of the broncho as it flies from the chute, and the experienced pony realizes this and makes sure that the rider cannot regain his rhythm. The bronchos have various methods of bucking and employ twists, turns and spirals in the effort to unseat the cowboys within the short time limit. The cowboys that fall try to roll clear of the still lashing hooves and are in danger of being badly kicked. After a successful ride a

bell heralds the end of the time limit and the cowboy dismounts either by grabbing the convenient rope around the top rail of the arena, or is aided by the two mounted ring-officials who ride alongside the broncho and help him off.

Other exciting events in the rodeo include bull-dogging and calf-roping. In bull-dogging a mounted cowboy has to catch a large steer and throw it. He relies on his mount greatly as this is a timed contest, the winner being the cowboy who throws his steer in the shortest time from the opening of the chute. The cowboy's pony leaps forward as the chute doors fling back and the steer appears, and gallops alongside the animal so that the cowboy can leap on to its back, clasp its horns and twist the huge beast to the ground. In calf-roping the pony plays an even more important part, for the rider first ropes the calf with his lasso and twists the loose-end around the saddle horn before he leaps to the ground. The pony is trained to back off to take up the slack enabling the rider to tie three of the calf's legs in the prescribed manner. The pony then walks towards the calf, slackening the rope so that it may be freed. Surprisingly, the calf does not seem to be disturbed by this rough handling, and returns to its penned companions quite unharmed.

A similar event is the calf-cutting, which calls for even more skill on the part of pony and cowboy alike. A bunch of calves is sent into the arena and the pony walks quietly into them on a loose rein. The cowboy selects a likely calf and indicates this to his pony, then the pony takes over and works the calf away from the rest of the herd, preventing it from running back to the others by intricate twists and turns. The pony must not receive any assistance or guidance whatsoever from its rider in this event, or the cowboy loses points. Having driven one calf away from the herd, the rider returns and selects another, and tries to show the prowess of his mount to the judges by selecting and cutting out three calves in the allotted time. The cutting ponies can anticipate every movement of the lively, skittish yearling calves. They move swiftly from side to side with almost

Ponies also enter with enthusiasm into pageants and parades and accept the indignity of being dressed up with surprising good grace.

dancing hooves and manoeuvre the calves with a grace and skill that is a fine testimony to their intelligence and to the expertise of their trainers.

Western-style riding classes and events have become popular in countries outside the United States, and some ponies have become very proficient in pole bending, barrel-racing and performing the special paces. Both ponies and riders must wear correct kit, which can vary slightly depending on the event entered. In the Western Pleasure class the pony is asked to walk, jog, then walk again before going into the lope. It must return smoothly to the walk, reverse and then repeat the movements on the other rein. The judges look for an equable temperament in the pony and free movement at all paces with smooth transitions between each change of gait.

In the Trail class the pony and rider have to complete a simulated trail ride and will be ex-

pected to walk, jog and lope as well as being asked to negotiate the obstacles often found along the normal trail. Six to eight obstacles are generally arranged in the ring and might include a latched gate to be opened, passed through and closed without dismounting. There will also be logs or straw bales to be dragged out of the path with the saddle rope, and poles or logs to be jumped, side-stepped and trotted over. Perhaps a wooden bridge to cross, car-tyres representing potholes to be negotiated and some form of tight gap to reverse through. Such contests really show the skill or otherwise of the pony and rider as well as the amount of training that has been given, and are popular with the audience who show their appreciation with much applause for a well-executed display.

Stock pony classes show the ability of the animal trained to work with cattle. The pony must be strong and well-made, heavy

Above
Riding bucking ponies in competitions calls for courage as well as riding skill for the bronchos know every trick there is for unseating even the best of riders. The cowboy must rely on balance alone to stay in the saddle and must not hold on with his hands or legs.

Above right
Peak fitness is essential in ponies competing in cloverleaf barrel-racing, which calls for tight turns at break-neck speed.

Right
The pony's role is critical in the sport of steer-wrestling for it manoeuvres the animal so that the cowboy can accurately time his leap.

enough to hold a steer on the rope, but agile enough to perform the lightning turns and twists which would be required for cutting cattle from a herd. In the ring, the pony performs without cattle and has to execute certain movements which show his training. From a standstill the pony must be able to break into a fast gallop for some 50 metres (164·5 feet), then slide, on its haunches to a standstill, forefeet lifted slightly off the ground. Then he must back a few steps before jogging across the arena to perform a series of intricate figure-of-eight movements. After riding to the centre of the ring the rider dismounts and lets the split rein ends dangle to the ground. This is known as ground-

tying and the pony must stand motionless while the rider walks away from him. After remounting, a simulated calf-roping display is performed before leaving the arena.

Cloverleaf barrel racing tests the turning ability and speed of the well-trained pony, for the event is run against the clock. The pony races through a timing-device beam and straight across the arena where it must turn sharply in a clockwise direction around a barrel before galloping over to the opposite side of the ring. Here the second barrel is rounded in an anti-clockwise direction, and the pony, still moving flat out, passes to the far end of the ground to the last

Above left
As the broncho plunges across the arena the rider tries to anticipate every change of direction.

Left
In calf-roping contests, the pony plays an important part in the proceedings for once the calf is lassoed, the pony stops dead and pulls back on the rope while the rider dismounts and ties the small animal's feet together.

Above
Pony trekking centres in many countries offer even inexperienced riders the opportunity to explore the surrounding areas at a pleasant pace from the unique vantage point afforded by a pony's back.

barrel. This is negotiated anti-clockwise and then a straight run back to the finishing-line completes the course. Good ponies can complete the course in very fast times, but certain penalties may be imposed by the judges. For example, the rider must not grasp the saddle horn or touch a barrel and only one hand may be used on the reins. Various other tests of the Western Pony's skill, speed, stamina and training may be offered at various shows and give immense enjoyment to the interested audience.

A more restful and less demanding way of leisure riding is afforded by pony trekking. This can be undertaken just for the odd day or for an holiday during which a large area of new or interesting country may be explored. Several countries have areas suitable for trekking, and establishments with docile, strong mounts

exist to take riders of all degrees of experience on wonderful mounted excursions through magnificent scenery. Ponies for trekking are well-schooled and hardy. They are comfortable to ride for long hours in the saddle and are selected for their sure-footedness over rough terrain. Trekking holidays are usually based in comfortable camps or hotels set among areas preserved as National Parks. Some treks take the form of daily excursions along different trails, returning to the base camp each evening to feed and rest the ponies before changing to enjoy an evening meal and entertainment before going to bed.

On some treks, the riding is over a continuous trail, with stops at different camps each night, sometimes in hotels, lodges or cabins or sometimes under canvas. Each rider is responsible for his own mount on such treks, but

A ride along a deserted beach at sunrise is surely the perfect way to begin each day of a riding holiday.

all equipment and extra clothing is usually transported ahead by truck to save overloading the ponies. In this way the riders can enjoy riding through different scenery each day and have their meals along the trail, but also benefit from a complete rest and change of clothes each evening. Even inexperienced riders soon become proficient as the trek progresses and learn to care for their ponies under the continuous and informal instruction along the route. The initial stiffness caused through using the muscles employed in riding soon wears off and the trek becomes really enjoyable.

In Iceland the typical Icelandic ponies are used for trekking through beautiful scenery with rugged icecaps, glaciers and bare, lava-covered mountain slopes as well as great tracts of prairie. In the spring many varieties of wild flowers bloom and the climate is perfect for a trekking holiday. The ponies used for trekking are well-made and strong and taught to amble along at a comfortable pace, known as the tølt, which is ideal for long-distance riding. The Icelandic treks pass rivers and lakes and the foothills of the volcanic mountains. Every evening is spent in eating a hearty meal and in singing traditional songs, and not surprisingly, many of these extol the virtues of the noble pony.

The Highlands of Scotland and the mountains of Wales provide ideal trekking areas, with their rugged tracks, acres of isolated riding country and long forest trails. Lots of wildlife can be observed from the backs of the sturdy trek ponies, which are equipped with comfortable tack, and are safe, docile mounts. British native ponies make ideal trekking animals, possessing great powers of endurance and having tractable natures. In Spain, local breeds are used for riding over spectacular trails through the mountains and along the river banks; the riders staying at small inns along the way.

Choosing and keeping a family pony

A good family pony may be of any shape or size, and need not be of any particular breed, but it must be fit and active, healthy and hardy enough to live out in a paddock all year. It must also be strong enough to carry all those members of the family that wish to ride and well-mannered enough to heed the light aids of the smallest equestrians of the family. Perhaps most important of all, it must have a kind, intelligent nature, and no really bad habits.

Small ponies are ideal for very small children who might feel unsafe on a larger animal, but the drawback to buying such small ponies is the fact that they are outgrown within two or three years, and small ponies are quite unsuitable for family use. A pony of 13 to 14 hands is generally large enough to carry the adult members of the family at slow paces, and small enough for a fairly young child to manage. Ponies of this size are usually inclined to better behaviour than the very small ones.

While it does not matter too much whether the family pony is very handsome, his conformation should be good enough to ensure that he moves with an action comfortable to his rider. A pony with a short, thick neck holds it in an awkward way, while one with a ewe-neck carries his head too high. Both types are uncomfortable to ride as they canter and

An equitable temperament is an important trait in the 'family pony' which happily tolerates all the other pets of the household.

A family pony should have good conformation like this well-made Connemara, with a short, strong back and good sloping shoulders.

jump in an ungainly manner. Straight shoulders in a pony give him a sharp jerking action at the trot, while some have insufficient space between their front legs, causing these to brush together and making the animal quite unsafe to ride. If the withers are not sufficiently developed, the saddle may slide forward when riding downhill, and if the back is long and straight, the saddle may well tend to slip back.

There are many ways to acquire a suitable family pony. Many magazines and papers which specialize in equine matters carry pages of advertisements describing ponies for sale. It is best, whenever possible, however, to buy a pony whose habits and history are known, either from friends or acquaintances, or on the recommendation of a veterinary surgeon. Novices should always take a knowledgeable friend along when trying out a new pony, and allow the friend to ride the animal at all paces as well as on the road. It is sometimes possible to take a pony home on trial for a week or so to ensure that it is wholly suitable. In any case it is usual and advisable to have the pony thor-

oughly checked by a veterinary surgeon before completing the purchase.

When selecting a pony, if possible see it being caught up from the field and watch while it is groomed and tacked-up. Some ponies are very difficult to catch and can cause frustrating delays when they are wanted for riding or for gymkhanas. Some ponies pretend to kick and bite when being groomed and tacked, while others kick and bite on purpose; the first sort are clowns and quite funny, the second sort can be lethal. It is a good idea to pick up the pony's feet one by one, for it is imperative that these can be properly attended to at all times. If the pony is unshod, it may mean that it has been turned away and the blacksmith has not yet called. It could mean that the pony is difficult or even impossible to shoe, and such ponies are obviously undesirable. The pony should stand quietly, ears pricked and alert while he is mounted, then move off promptly as the correct aids are applied. It is of the utmost importance to see how it reacts to being ridden along a busy road, for a traffic-shy pony is a menace to himself and every

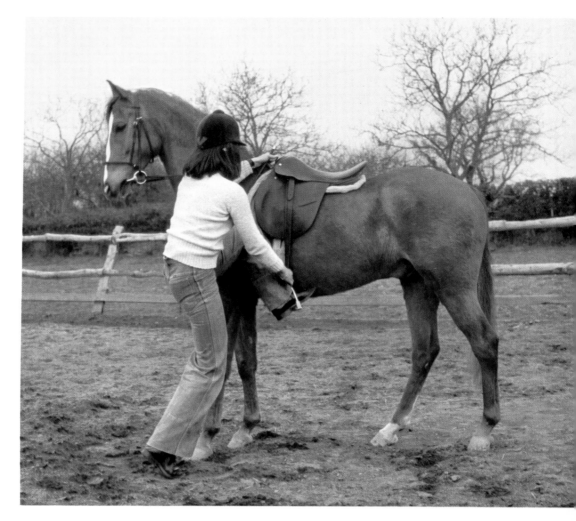

Right
When trying out a new pony it is important that he stands quietly, while being mounted, until the rider is seated correctly in the saddle.

Below right
He can then be rewarded with a pat.

other road user. When trying the pony, it should be ridden at all paces and possibly put over a low jump. It should be observed whether or not it goes as willingly away from its stable as on the return, and whether or not it objects to being ridden away from other ponies. If you are hoping to enter gymkhanas or other events, it is advisable to ask if you may see the pony led into a horsebox or trailer.

Geldings are probably the best ponies for general family use although mares are said to be more intelligent and affectionate. However, mares can be a problem when they come in season. It is really impossible to generalize on which is better, for any pony owner of longstanding will tell you of delightfully affectionate geldings and equally troublefree mares.

Young ponies are not really suitable for novice riders, although their attraction may be in their reasonable price tags. Very old ponies may not be capable of doing all the work required of a family pony although they might prove ideal for a small or nervous child, being quiet, reliable and docile. The best age for a family

pony is between seven and twelve years, when it will be old enough to be sensible and young enough to spend several happy years in the same home. A pony of suitable height, aged about four years and carefully broken in, but not yet schooled may be more reasonably priced, and provided that the home is a knowledgeable one, he could turn out to be the ideal family mount. Ponies may grow until they reach the age of five or six and these years are the formative ones, important both mentally and physically.

If the field has a flowing stream running through it, the pony may drink from this, but water in small stagnant ponds is likely to be polluted and may make the animal ill. Containers used for water should be sturdy and unlikely to cut the pony's legs if they are tipped over. Although, for most of the year, grass is an adequate feed for the pony, it will need supplementary feeding in the winter months, and unless performing hard or strenuous work such as hunting, hay is usually satisfactory. Hay should be fed to the family pony from the onset of the colder months through until the new spring

grasses appear. It should be packed into a rope haynet and tied at a height equal to that of the pony's shoulder. If it is tied up too high, the pony may get dust and seeds in its eyes, and if it is too low, it may get its feet entangled in the mesh. If the summer is long and hot without rain, it may be necessary to give supplementary feeding to compensate for the lack of grass, and specially formulated cubes are available for ponies. In the winter, the occasional hot bran mash may be given, especially after the pony has had extra work.

If the pony is turned out to rest for any length of time, its shoes should be removed. The blacksmith should trim back the hooves about every five or six weeks to keep them in good condition. When in regular work the pony's feet must be cared for by daily inspection and picking out any stones or dirt caught between the frog and the shoe. The shoes should be attended to regularly by a good blacksmith and never allowed to become too worn down or loose before being changed.

There seems to be a current vogue among families with little or no knowledge of ponies to

Above
The pony should be tried at all paces to see that he goes forward freely on either rein.

Above right
He must stand quietly again while the rider dismounts and runs up the stirrups.

Right
It is also important that a pony is easy to lead and goes forward freely on a loose rein, alongside his handler.

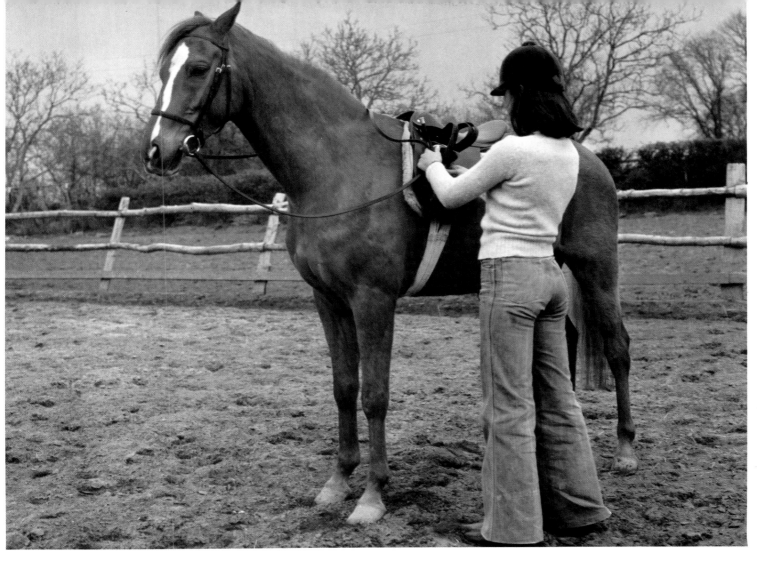

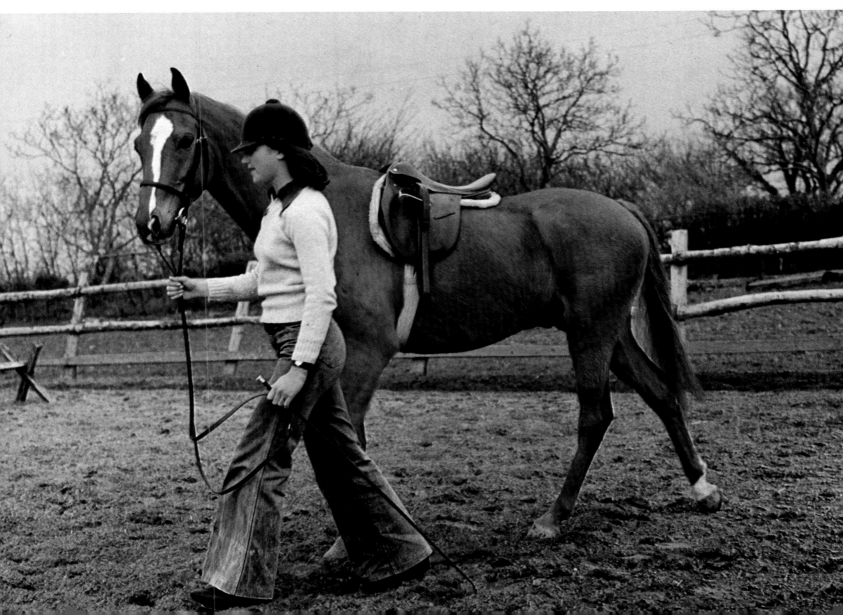

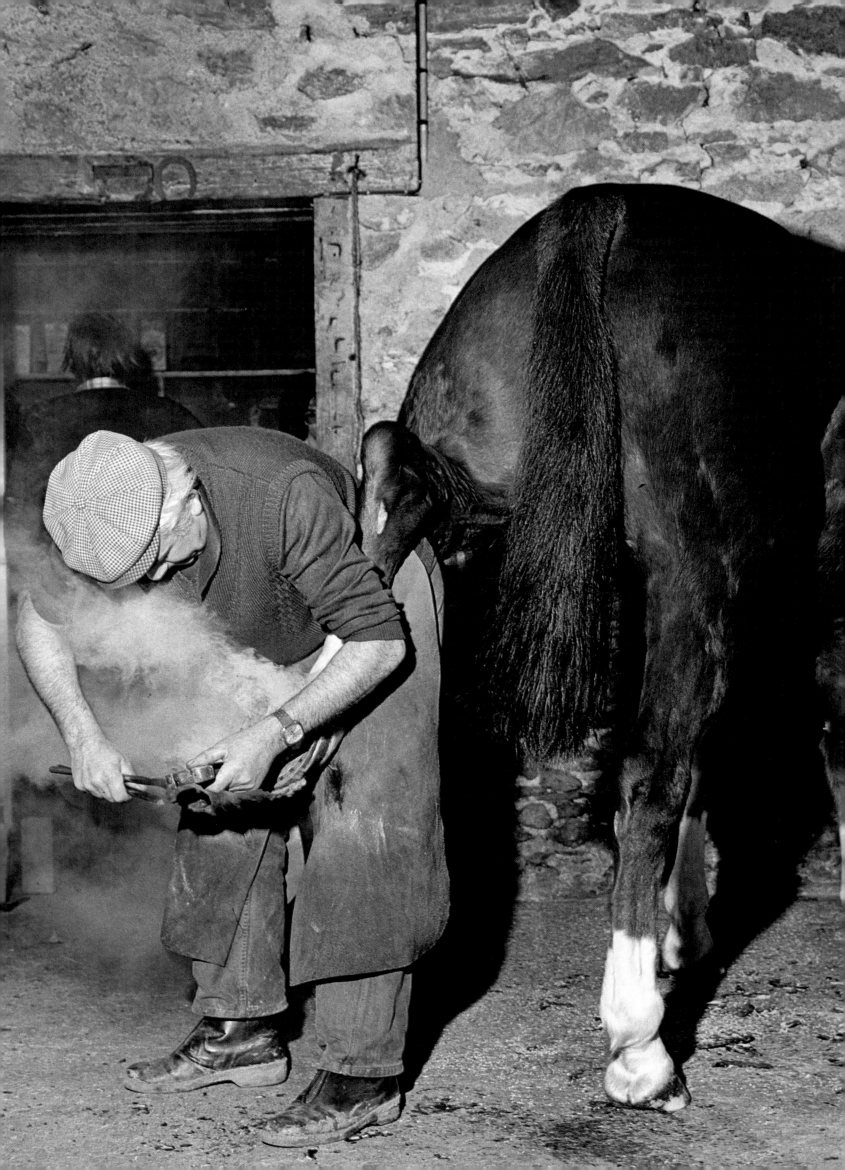

Left
The regular attentions of a qualified blacksmith are essential for all ponies, for their hooves must be kept in good order at all times. Loose or ill-fitting shoes can be very dangerous and may cause the pony to come down on the road, perhaps in heavy traffic, with disastrous consequences.

Above
The family pony will benefit from being put into a cool stable away from biting insects on hot summer days and can be turned out again to graze through the night.

attend horsefairs and sales and to come home with a foal in the back of the car. Such foals can be purchased for very low cost and are then kept in the back garden, being fed on scraps. Sooner or later the foal breaks through the inadequate fencing and, if it is lucky, steps are taken to find a local farmer who will let it live in a safe field. The children of the family sometimes lose interest in the little animal, when it may be sold and find itself in better circumstances. All too often though, groups of children, all proud owners of such youngsters, tire of waiting for the ponies to mature and start to ride them. Narrow-chested, badly reared young ponies bearing unsuitable, ill-fitting tack, can be seen being ridden along grass verges outside towns by children for whom the animal is a substitute bicycle.

The responsible family who decide to buy a pony will ensure that they have sufficient knowledge to look after it properly, and if they are inexperienced, that they have reliable friends to whom they may turn for help and advice when necessary. They will have made certain of the costs of all aspects of pony care including feeding, housing, equipment, shoeing and veterinary attention. This sort of family deserves a good all-round pony which will repay all the care and attention lavished upon it with many years of willing and faithful service.

A well-fenced grass field is the ideal place to keep a family pony, and if it has a draught-proof shelter to allow the pony to rest away from flies and midges in the summer, so much the better. A suitable water container which can be cleaned out regularly is essential in the field, for a pony must have fresh water at all times. If buckets have to be used, these should be stood within a small car tyre.

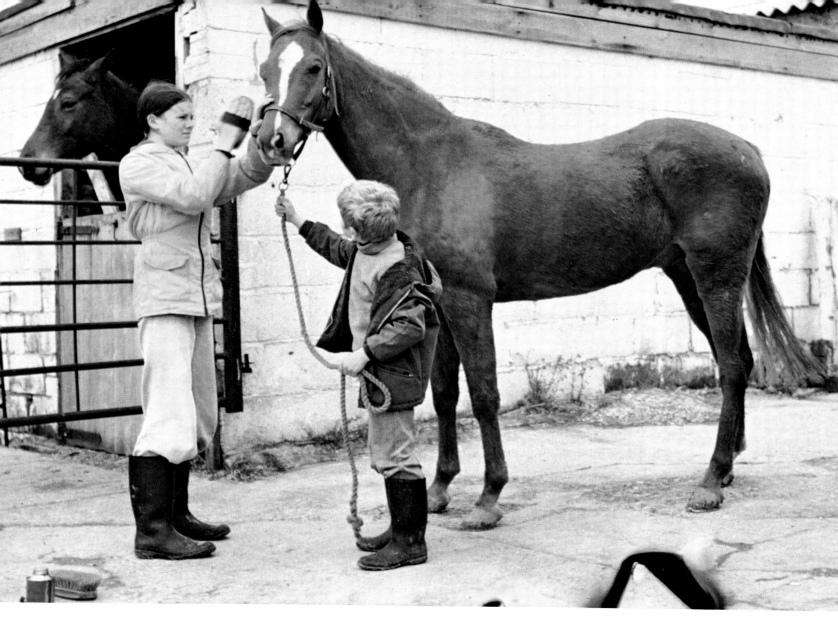

The pony which lives out all the year round must be allowed to grow a natural, thick winter coat, and in the winter, after hard work which has raised a sweat, it must be thoroughly dried off before being turned out into the field. The pony will often find the muddiest part of its field to roll in and coat its body as a protection against the weather, which makes it extremely hard work to get ready for a ride the following day. Only the surface mud should be brushed away to prevent any soreness developing when it is tacked-up and ridden. The natural oil and grease deep down in the hair near the roots must be left, as this protects the pony living out at grass. After riding, the areas which have been in contact with the saddle and bridle should be briskly rubbed to restore the circulation and to prevent galls from forming in the skin.

Ponies need regular worming treatments which can be prescribed by the veterinary surgeon and are extremely important if they are to be kept in good health.

The droppings in the field should also be gathered up occasionally, or if dry, spread with a rake. The area where the pony stands to rest, whether or not it is in a shelter, should not be muddy or the animal may develop cracked heels. A thick straw mat can be spread in such areas. The field should be inspected now and again to ensure that no plants poisonous to the pony have grown through, and any strange new plant should be identified to make sure that it is harmless if eaten by the pony.

Some ponies are difficult to catch and so should be turned out wearing a well-fitting leather or nylon headcollar with safe buckles and fastenings. Shy ponies should be caught at various and irregular intervals and not only at times when they will be worked. In this way they will soon stop expecting hard work every time they are approached and instead will come to associate the act of being caught with being given an appetizing small feed and some enjoyable grooming. Ponies are definitely happier if turned out in

Above
The family pony should be lightly groomed each day while being tied-up or held by a rope attached to his headcollar. When his summer coat is through he only needs the loose hair and mud to be brushed away to make him presentable for normal work. First, his face and forelock are gently brushed clean.

Above right
Then the nearside of his neck and shoulder and his near or left foreleg are groomed.

Right
His back, flank and belly are brushed next, followed by the quarters and down the near hind leg.

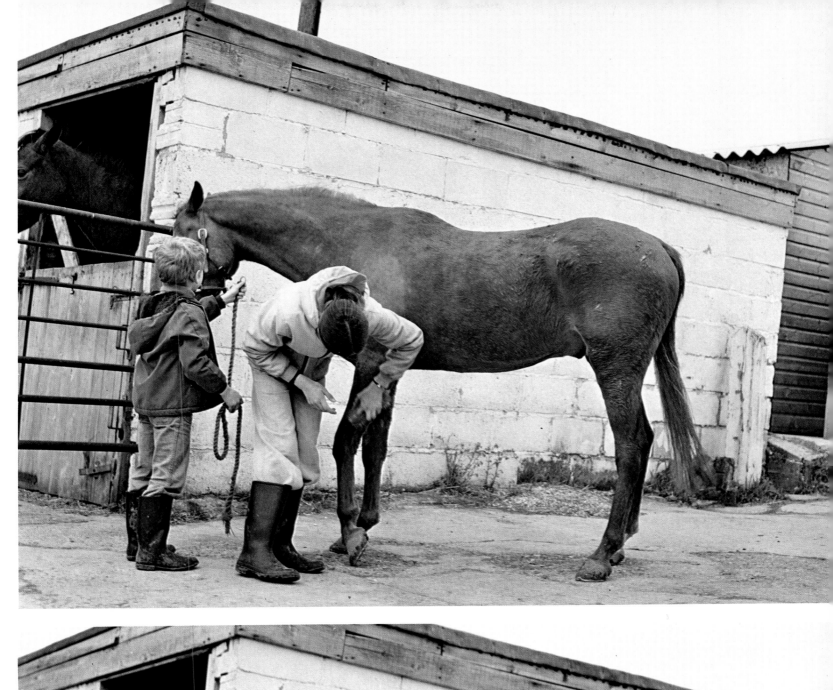
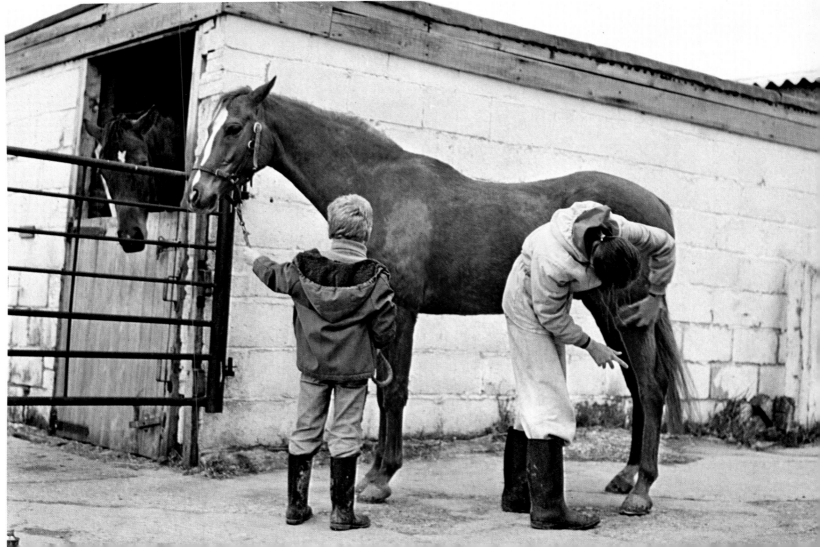

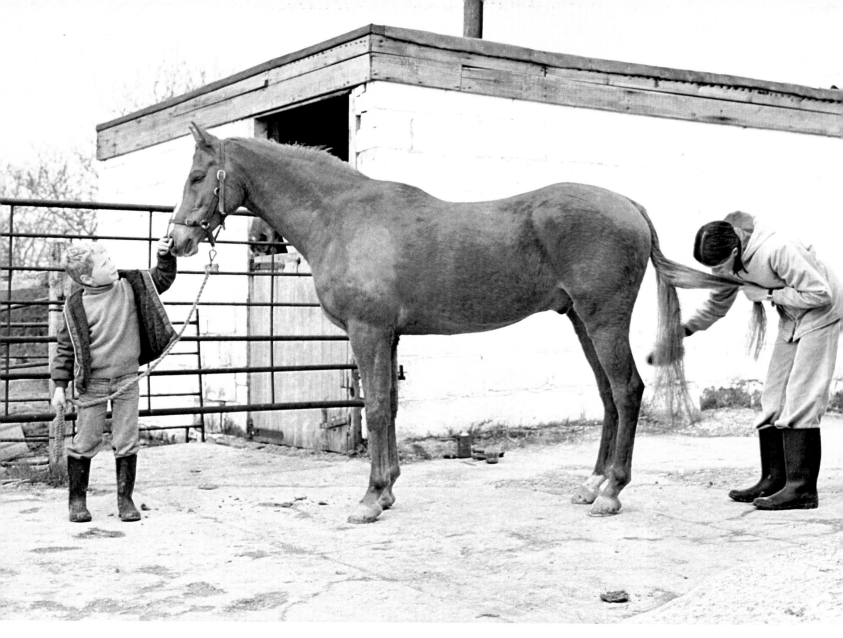

After treating the offside of the pony in exactly the same manner, plus a thorough brushing of the mane which falls on that side of the neck, the tail is brushed out. This is done strand by strand until each hair falls clean and separated into place.

company for they are natural herd animals; however, not all ponies get on well together. It is very important to feed ponies separately in the field, tying the haynets well apart, for ponies can kick and bite each other jealously over food. When a strange pony is introduced, much squealing and mock fighting breaks out and the ponies must be watched in case of trouble, but they usually settle down and form a happy, peaceful group.

The most important aspect of keeping the family pony at grass is to ensure that the fences or hedges and gates are completely pony-proof. Ponies are notorious for their Houdini-like characteristics and will push through any weak part of a hedge. Post-and-rail fences are the best for ponies although they are quite expensive, and many people have to make do with wire. Wire, whether barbed or plain, must be very taut and fixed to stout stakes. The bottom wire must be high enough to prevent the pony from getting

his foot over it and becoming caught up. Gates must be secure and as easy to open as they are to close, for it is tricky trying to cope with an excited pony and a jammed gate. Given enough to eat, a pony will be happy and contented within its field, and if it is large enough it should be divided so that each section gets some rest to recover from the pony's inefficient grazing techniques. The ideal area would be about two acres, divided into two, and big enough for two friendly family ponies to share.

Just as it is important to make sure your pony is well-fed in the winter, it is equally important to prevent it over-eating on the lush summer grass. The easiest methods of testing the pony for good condition are simple, first lay your hand flat over his ribs and move it gently back and forth. The flesh should move too and not feel stiff and taut. The other place to test is the crest of the neck; if it feels flabby and thin when gripped in the hand, the

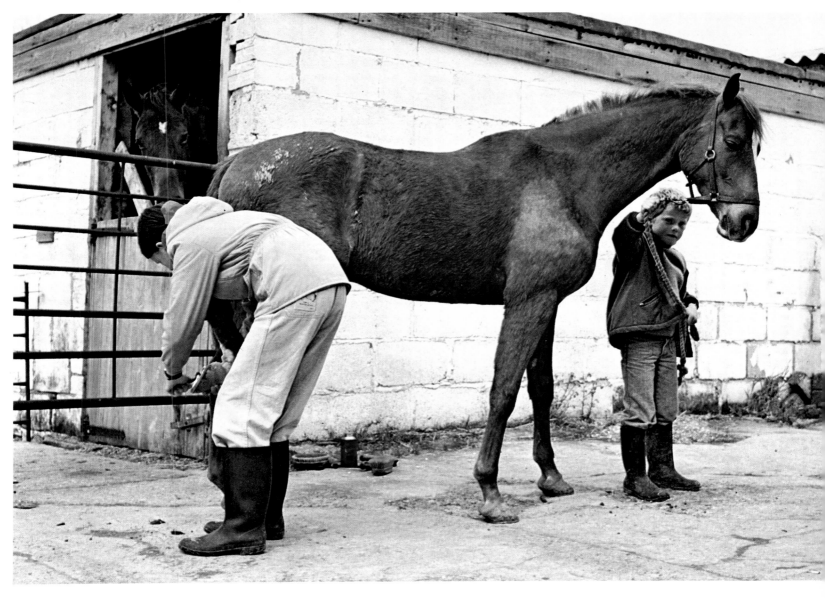

Whether the family pony is ridden each day or not, his feet should be regularly examined, and the first thing to be done after catching him up from the field is to pick out mud, grit or stones from the hooves using a specially designed hoof pick.

pony is in poor condition, and if it feels extremely hard and difficult to squeeze, the pony is too fat. It is bad for grass-fed ponies to be allowed to get grossly overweight. Some ponies are prone to a distressing condition known as laminitis, which is an inflammation of the feet and very painful. Greedy ponies which are allowed to gorge on new spring grass are the most prone to this condition which can lame the animal for many months. The best method of restricting the grazing during the spring and early summer is to confine the pony within a stable, shed or shelter during the day and turn it out only at night. This will also help the animal to rest away from biting flies and insects on hot days. While confined, the pony must have plenty of water and possibly a rock salt or mineral lick.

The pony at grass should not have its mane and tail trimmed too much for the tail acts as an efficient fly switch and the mane and long forelock protect the

pony's face and neck from biting insects. Regular brushing will keep the mane and tail in good condition and uneven, ragged pieces should be carefully pulled out from the roots and never cut to shape with scissors. Unless the pony is to be shown and must be smartened up for the ring, a full mane and tail kept well brushed in this way is quite tidy enough for everyday riding. Any long hairs on the fetlocks can be carefully trimmed with scissors for this makes it easier to clean the legs after a muddy ride.

The grass-fed pony should be caught up and tied while he is brushed down and tacked-up, and must not be fed or watered before starting work. On the return from the ride, the girth should be undone but the saddle left on while the pony cools down. It may be given a drink of water, but if the animal is hot and sweaty, the water should have the chill taken off by adding some from a boiled kettle. After drinking and cooling off, the pony can

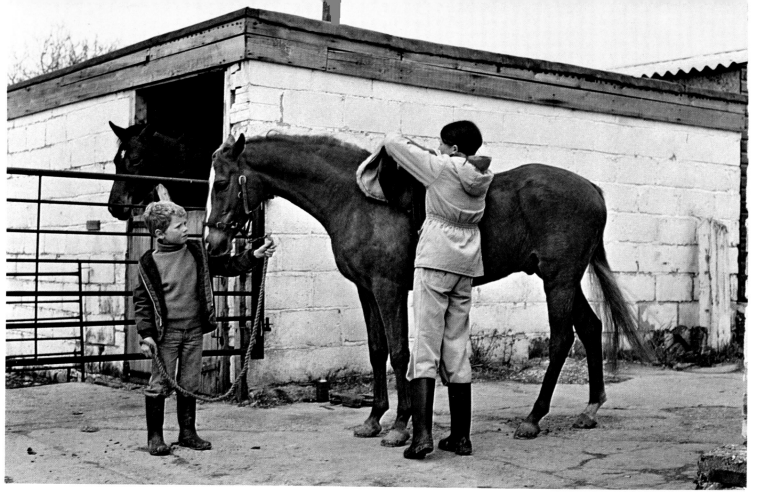

When tacking-up, the saddle is first placed well forward on the pony's withers before being slid back into place. This makes sure that all the hairs are lying flat.

have its well-deserved feed, or be turned out to graze.

While the grass-fed family pony will give much enjoyment and pleasure, a pony used for more serious riding, showing, regular hunting or for strenuous jumping contests should be kept stabled so that it can be given extra work and rations. Such a pony can be completely clipped out in winter and kept in a fit and hard condition at all times. Obviously such a pony must be treated differently to the grass-fed pony which spends most of its time quietly grazing in the field. The stabled pony is a creature of routine and it is important to keep to regular and punctual habits when looking after him. Feeding, grooming and exercise periods should all follow a set pattern.

First thing each morning, the pony's water bucket must be taken from his stable and rinsed out before refilling it with fresh, clean water. When the pony has had his drink he can be haltered and tied up with a small feed. His nightrug may have become stretched or shifted during the night, or pulled back so that it is cutting into the withers, so it should be readjusted for his comfort during his breakfast. While he is eating, the soiled bedding can be quietly removed and the dry material heaped around the

sides of the loosebox walls. The pony will happily move over while the box floor is swept clean and all the debris is moved outside. A little of the clean bedding is shaken on the floor, then the pony can be untied and left with a small haynet.

Later on the pony has his rug removed and put with the inside facing outwards to air. The pony is then thoroughly strapped, either in the box or out in the sunshine if it is a fine, warm day. First any dirt or mud left on from the previous day must be carefully removed with the stiff dandy brush, starting at the head and working down the neck and shoulder, then down the foreleg. The pony is brushed over the saddlemark and along the back, then the quarters, flank and down the hind leg. The other side is treated in the same way and the loose hairs are pulled from the brush and placed neatly in a bucket or bin. The brushing procedure is then repeated using the soft body brush which is designed to muscle up the pony as well as to impart a gloss to his coat. Using the body brush is vigorous work, and is performed in long strokes using the arm nearest the side being groomed, and with the whole weight of the body behind the motion. After every five or six strokes the brush is wiped across

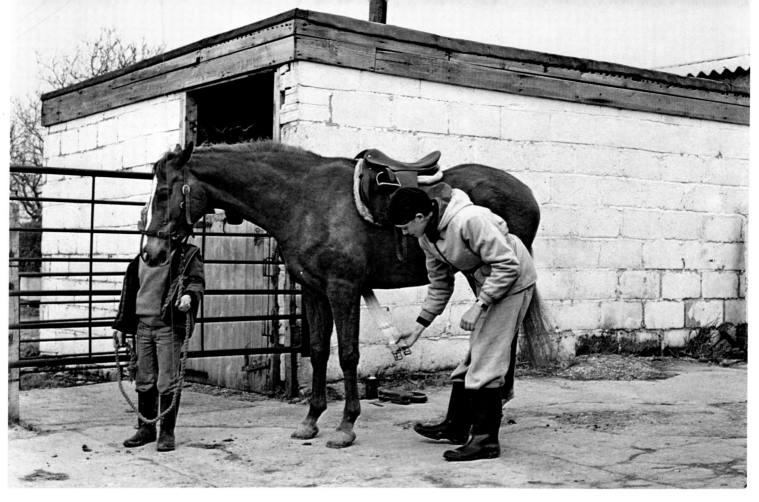

Then the girth is passed under the belly and strapped to the saddle.

the blades of the specially designed currycomb which is held in the other hand. This removes scurf and dust from the brush and can be knocked out into the bin as this collects. It is important to learn to use the body brush correctly as this is the instrument for keeping the correctly fed, stabled pony in tiptop condition as well as improving his general appearance.

The mane and tail of the stabled pony are kept in shape by regular pulling. The extra hair of the mane is reduced by removing hairs from underneath. The mane is parted lengthwise and a small tuft is selected at the withers end. This is fluffed towards his neck with a mane comb and the remaining long hairs are twisted around the comb and jerked out. Only a few hairs must be taken at a time so that the pony is not hurt or he may come to resent the operation. The procedure is repeated along the length of the mane, then the top layer is brushed down. With practise, the mane can be kept neat and trim.

The tail is trimmed by pulling the odd hairs from the side of the dock and the bottom of the tail can be banged, which means it is cut off at the bottom at such an angle that it hangs neatly and squarely when the pony holds it out in its natural position. The

mane and tail are thoroughly brushed through each day so that every hair is clean and separate.

Care of the pony's feet is essential and part of the grooming procedure is to lift each hoof and use a hoof-pick to remove all the material that has collected in the area between the frog and the shoe. The hoof-pick is made of pointed metal and must be used carefully so as not to damage the sole of the hoof. To pick up the pony's feet the hand is run down the shoulder or quarters and then to the fetlock. Most ponies are trained to lift the foot when the fetlock is squeezed, or they are told to 'come up'. The hoof is held in one hand and the pick is used to scrape either side of the soft, rubbery frog from the heel towards the toe. When picking out the feet the shoes should be checked, for riding a pony with loose or worn shoes can be very dangerous.

The pony should visit the blacksmith every four or five weeks, and if the shoes are not worn they can be removed so that the extra, newly grown horn can be cut back to shape before the shoes are re-fitted. The best method of shoeing is the 'hot' method, but more and more blacksmiths fit cold shoes these days. By the hot shoeing method, the blacksmith manufactures the

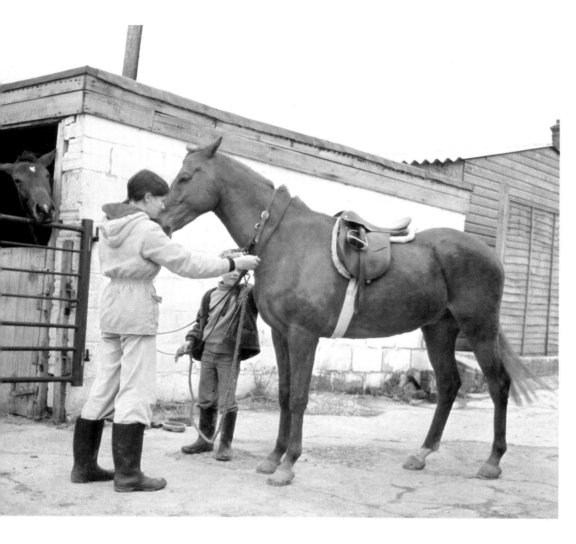

Left
Next the bridle reins are passed over the pony's neck and the headcollar is removed before the bit is put in his mouth.

Below left and far right
Then the headpiece of the bridle is passed over the pony's ears and his forelock pulled to hang free.

Below right
All the bridle straps must be done up carefully and the ends tucked neatly in their keepers.

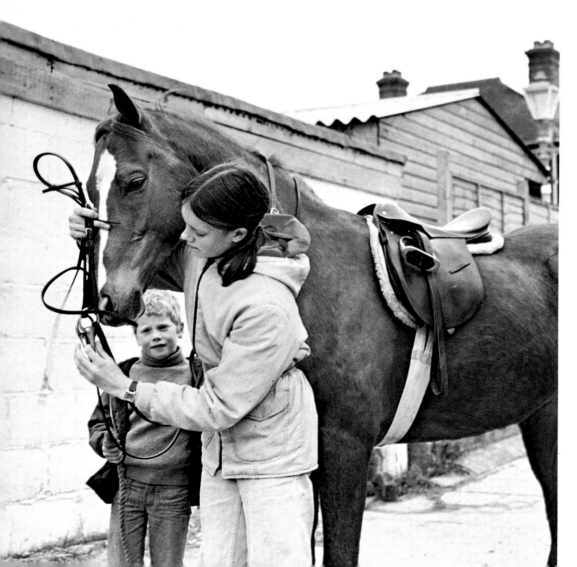

iron shoes from bars of metal and constructs them to exactly fit the pony's feet, hammering the hot iron to shape until he is completely satisfied, heating and re-heating the metal in the forge fire. When they are completely right, he tempers the shoes by plunging them in cold water before nailing them to the pony's insensitive horny hooves.

In cold shoeing, the blacksmith has many different sizes and shapes of shoes available and tries these against the pony's trimmed hooves until he finds the best fit. The shoes are nailed on, then any superfluous horn is trimmed away. By this method the foot is made to fit the shoe, while in the hot method, as we have seen, the shoe is made to fit the foot, which is obviously much better. The pony may have special hoof oil applied to each foot before going for a ride, and if he is prone to brittle hooves, this treatment is beneficial. However, it is usually applied only to improve the pony's appearance, and the hooves should be clean and dry before it is brushed on.

When tacking-up, the pony is tied or held while the saddle is put on several inches in advance

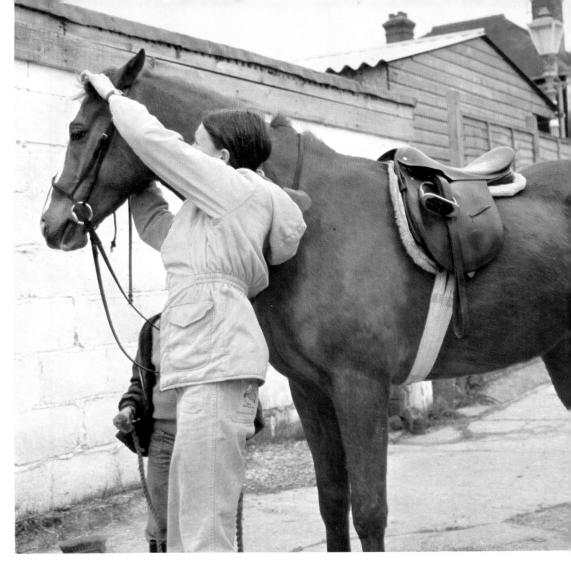

of its correct position. It is then slid gently back into place so that the hairs of the back lie comfortably flat beneath it. A saddle pad, blanket or numnah can be used as a pad under the saddle if the pony is young, thin or has a tender or narrow back. The girth is fastened underneath the pony's belly but should not be tightened at first until the saddle has had a chance to warm up and settle on his back. Next the reins of the bridle are passed over the pony's head so that he can be safely held while the head collar is taken off. Holding the headpiece of the bridle in the right hand, the bit is pressed gently against the pony's teeth until he opens his mouth to accept it, then the headpiece is passed over the ears and into place. The various straps are fastened so that the bridle is safely and comfortably fitted and care must be taken to see that none of the leatherwork chafes or rubs against the ears or the projecting cheek bones. Nosebands must not restrict the pony's breathing in any way.

All tack must be looked after carefully and inspected regularly so that any parts which wear can be repaired. Girths and stirrup

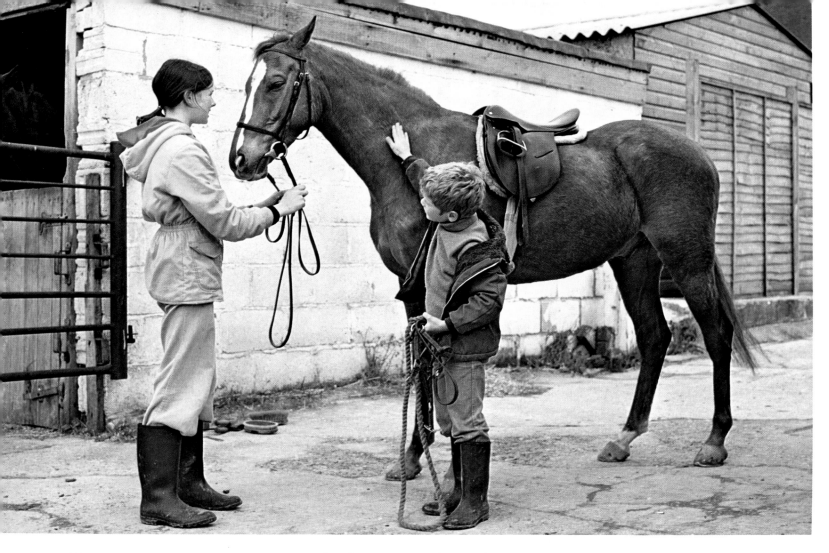

Finally a quick check is made to ensure that the tack is fitted comfortably and the pony is given a pat for standing so quietly.

leathers must always be strong, for the rider's life depends on the strength and safety of such equipment. Stirrup leathers should be adjusted by one hole either way from time to time so that the area which passes through the iron is varied. The girth straps on the saddle should be checked every time the saddle is used and the stitching must be attended to as soon as it looks loose or frayed. All leather work should be washed free from dirt and sweat straight after a ride, then when it is dry, soft saddle soap is rubbed well in with a wet sponge. After being allowed to dry the leather can be buffed up with a soft cloth. When cleaning the bridle, all the buckles should be undone and particular attention paid to the areas of straps which pass through the buckles as these must be kept in good order and very supple. Reins must also be soaped well and kept in good condition, being replaced or professionally mended at the first signs of wear. If the tack is methodically cleaned every time it is used, it is always ready for the next ride and will also last for many years. Neglected tack deteriorates rapidly and as well as being dangerous in use, is expensive to replace.

The pony's rugs must also be well looked after and aired well each day. It is usual for the pony to have jute night rugs which can be aired all day, and smart woollen day rugs which are aired at night. Loose hairs are brushed from the insides of the rugs before they are replaced on the pony. In very cold weather a clipped pony may have the extra comfort of a warm blanket underneath the rugs.

After the morning exercise the pony must be returned home free from sweat, and to achieve this, should be quietly walked for the last half kilometre (half mile) or so. If the pony is very fit, however, or still too fresh and jogs skittishly home he may well arrive back at the stable in a very hot state. If this is the case, his feet should be washed out in the yard; then he can be tied in his box while he is banged and dried with a wisp of soft hay. His ears should be dried with the stable rubber and he must be thoroughly dried out before he is rugged-up. A hot pony should only be given a small drink and the water must have the chill taken off by the addition of some hot water to the bucket. When he has settled and had his drink he may be fed and bedded

When stabled, a pony with a thin coat may need extra protection from the cold. On return from exercise, he is cooled off, then after brushing down, a stable blanket is thrown over his back.

down for the rest of the day. At teatime the droppings are removed from the stable and a further period of exercise can be undertaken if desired. After this the pony is very thoroughly strapped before his night feed is given and his night rug is put on.

Each pony requires different feeding, so it is impossible to generalize. Ponies in different countries are fed quite different mixtures of cereals and grains. It is important to remember, however, that all ponies require a considerable amount of bulk and need feeding little and often rather than at one large session. A

pony in good condition is sure to be getting the right amount and quantity of food and will be neither too fat nor too thin. He will be gay and alert and his coat will shine. Most ponies eat a large proportion of hay in their diets, and this must be fresh and sweet-smelling, not musty and full of dust. Sometimes hay and straw are finely chopped together to form chaff which is excellent for bulking out the pony's concentrates and grain. Bran is made into an appetizing mash when covered with boiling water and allowed to stand until cool.

If the pony is listless or his coat

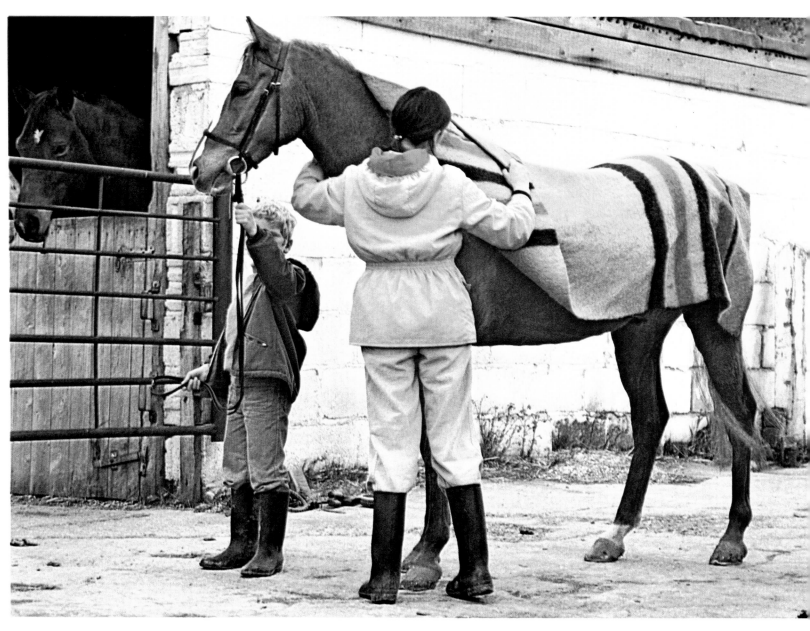

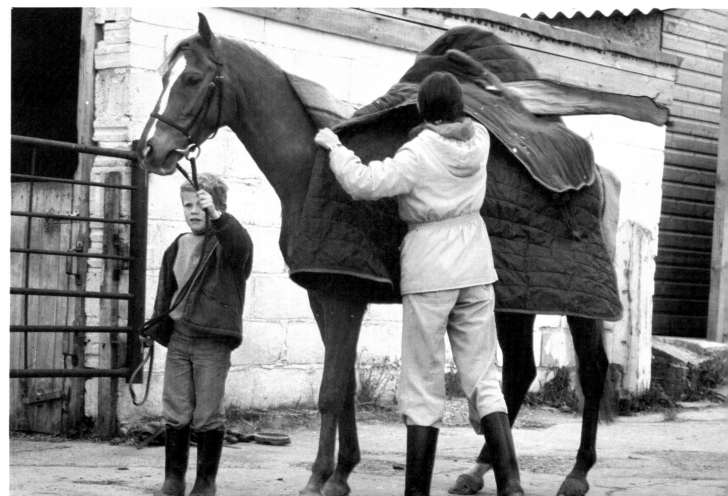

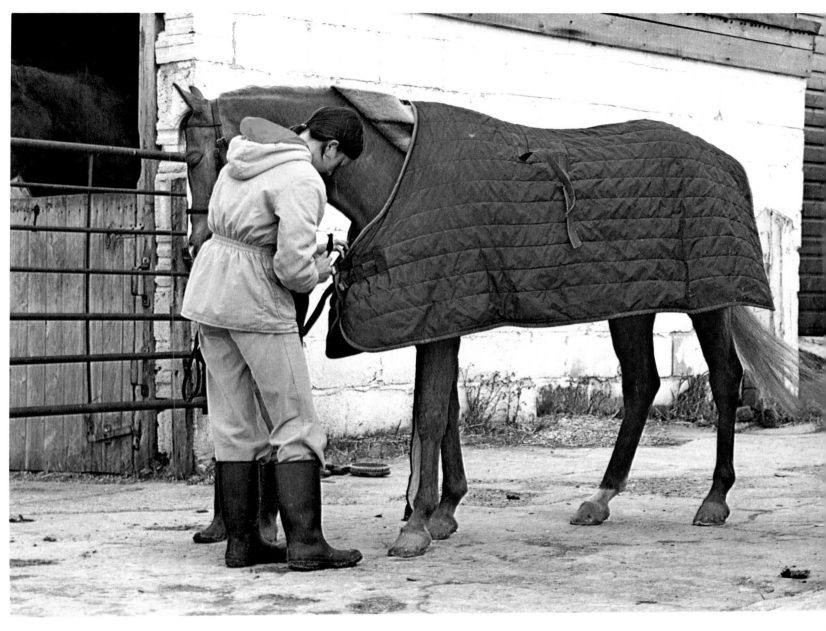

Above left
It is carefully positioned and folded to fit his back and withers.

Left
A rug is put on top of the blanket and the front straps are buckled so that the pony has plenty of freedom to move around.

Above
The belly-straps are fastened snugly and the pony is given a pat. It is always important to reward ponies in this way when they have been patient and well-behaved.

looks dull, he probably suffers from internal parasites. Ponies should be dosed against worms at regular intervals in any case, for they are particularly prone to these pests. A dung sample should be collected and taken to the veterinary surgeon for examination and he will soon be able to suggest the correct vermifuge for the pony. Most ponies are easy to dose and the remedial powder can be sprinkled into the normal feed. Other ponies are suspicious and leave the food. In this case the pony should be allowed to go hungry for several hours, then the small feed complete with powder and lots of brown sugar can be offered, when the pony should accept it readily. Leaving food may indicate that the pony is having some trouble in the mouth and the veterinary surgeon should have a look at his teeth. Sometimes the teeth grow jagged and uneven and need filing down with a large rasp. Very occasionally a

tooth has to be removed, and after such treatment the pony usually starts to put on condition quite rapidly.

Ponies are very strong and, when well cared for, keep healthy and fit most of the time. Should the pony suffer from runny eyes or a wet nose he may have picked up a cold from another pony. Strange as it may seem, ponies kept out at grass are less prone to this type of infection than their stabled companions. The eyes and nose must be sponged regularly and kept free from caked matter, and if the pony develops a fever, the veterinary surgeon must be called without delay. Any pony which develops a cough must be rested, for riding a coughing pony could ruin his wind and make him useless for normal riding in the future. Coughing is usually treated with a cough mixture which is added to the feed once or twice a day, and the addition of molasses or honey to the diet is also beneficial.

Schooling and showing

To really enjoy riding your pony it is essential to understand the basic aspects of riding, why certain aids are applied and how to get the best out of your mount. To help this understanding perhaps it is advisable to learn how the pony walks, trots, canters, gallops and jumps, and how he can be helped to perform all these movements smoothly and comfortably, at all times. Most ponies walk well, covering the ground easily with long swinging strides, ears pricked, eyes looking all around for anything that might be of interest. Ponies like this are a pleasure to ride for little effort is required to keep them moving freely forward. A pony with an energetic, free walk is likely to be equally generous and bold at other paces, always eager to give of his best. A pony that is lethargic at the walk is likely to be equally sluggish when asked to perform his other paces and can be frustrating to ride.

Movement in the pony is governed by the action of the shoulders, and in choosing a pony, set-back sloping shoulders are the type to look for as these will produce the desired long, swinging stride. Straight, upright shoulders cause the pony to move mainly with the action of the knees and therefore at all paces the movement will be short and jerky, and tiring for both rider and mount. As the pony walks, each foot should be distinctly lifted, moved forward and placed down in a decisive, firm way, without any sign of shuf-

Above
The lunge-rein here is attached to a leather cavesson (noseband) worn by the pony as it is encouraged to jump a series of cavaletti placed in a wide circle. This exercise teaches the pony to be accurate and well-balanced before going on to take proper jumps.

Left
This well-schooled pony is moving forward well with plenty of impulsion while its rider retains proper contact with the reins.

fling, either brushing the toes against the ground or the inside of the hooves against each other. It must be remembered, however, that a very young or immature pony, or one that is unfit, may drag its toes, whereas with schooling and good feeding it will improve its action considerably. The young pony that drags its feet at the walk should be trotted on hard ground when the action of the knees should stop the toes dragging.

The trot is probably the most important pace for testing a pony's action and soundness, for it reveals whether or not the action is straight, and whether the pony 'dishes' or 'plaits'. In dishing, the pony throws its feet outwards and in plaiting they are thrown inwards, and both conditions cause the pony to be uncomfortable to ride. Plaiting is particularly serious for the pony can trip himself and fall, and is therefore dangerous to himself and his rider. Other parts of the pony's legs, such as the knee or fetlock joint may brush together if the pony has bad conformation. These defects may be corrected by fitting the pony with specially made

shoes; they sometimes correct themselves as the pony grows to maturity. Trotting a pony on a hard road will immediately show up any form of lameness for not only can the action be seen to falter, but the even cadence of the sound is broken.

In the walk the pony moves its limbs in four-time, the hooves being placed down in sequence – off-fore, near-hind, near-fore, off-hind – while in the trot the legs move alternately on two diagonals and thus it is a pace in two-time. The right diagonal movement has the off-fore and the near-hind moving together, while the left diagonal consists of the near-fore and the off-hind. There is a short suspension period between the two diagonal movements. The trot, as the walk, can be either natural, collected or extended, and in some countries sophisticated versions of the trot are taught to ponies which have to cover long distances at a brisk pace without becoming tired. The natural walk and trot are used in hacking and are comfortable paces for covering the ground economically. It is interesting to note that in the wild, ponies

rarely seem to trot, seeming to prefer to walk or canter; exceptions to this rule are the Dartmoor and Exmoor Ponies which do trot in herds from one grazing area to another.

When riding at the trot there are two methods of coping with the rather uncomfortable action. The action can 'sit' to the trot which gives him very close contact with the pony and enables him to control its movements more precisely. This method can be very uncomfortable on ponies with a short, choppy action, or at the extended trot, and can quickly tire the rider. On a smooth, slow trotting pony it can be a relaxed and enjoyable way to ride. The other method is to 'rise' to the trot and the rider lifts himself very slightly out of the saddle on the first beat of the pace and lowers himself gently on the second beat. With practice this becomes an effortless, graceful movement. When the rider sits back in the saddle as the pony's near-fore and off-hind strike the ground he is said to be riding on the left diagonal; when he sits down as the off-fore and near-hind strike, he is said to be riding on the right diagonal. Some ponies prefer to be ridden on a

particular diagonal at the trot and will shy or break stride in an effort to make the rider change the diagonal. A well-schooled pony will accept being ridden on either diagonal, and a good rider will change occasionally to encourage this.

The trot is the fastest pace at which a pony should be worked on the road or any other hard surface, for the sake of safety and to prevent jarring of his legs. Trotting uphill at a slow pace is the perfect exercise for getting a pony well-muscled and fit; young ponies should receive daily lungeing and circling at the trot to teach suppleness and balance. Most ponies are schooled over a

line of cavaletti – low jumping poles, spaced equally apart. Trotting down such a line teaches the pony to accurately place each foot and to lift his knees and hocks correctly.

Perhaps the most difficult pace for both pony and rider to comfortably unite is the canter. This is a pace of three-time in which one pair of fore- and hind-legs leads, or strikes the ground, in front of the other pair. The leading leg is the term applied to whichever foreleg strikes the ground first. It is usual for a pony cantering in a circle to lead with the leg describing the inside of that circle; this enables him to keep his balance. In this way a

Before going to the collecting ring, the show pony is carefully prepared. His mane and tail are plaited and his hooves painted with oil, to enhance his appearance.

pony cantering in a left-handed circle is said to be leading with the near-fore. When cantering correctly in this way, the canter is described as being united, but occasionally a pony will lead with the near-fore and the off-hind and is then said to be cantering dis-united and is extremely uncomfortable to ride. With practise, and a well-schooled fluent pony, the canter can be a joy. The rider learns to sit well down in the saddle, to relax his back and to allow his body to pivot from the tightly gripped knees, so that the fluid motion of the cadenced strides swing his upper body to the motion of the pony. Some ponies use the comparative freedom of the canter to indulge in some mock rodeo tactics, and if too fit, or if the day is excitingly

windy, may decide to buck or shy, or deliberately try to unseat their riders. For this reason it is important to maintain proper contact with the pony's mouth and to start the cantering session in a controlled fashion. Young ponies when being schooled are rarely taught any movements at the canter, and then only when the manoeuvres have been thoroughly mastered at the trot.

The gallop is not merely a fast canter for it is a pace of four-time, and is the fastest speed at which a pony can move. No pony should be galloped for long distances, but the fit animal will be capable of galloping on gamely when out hunting. At the gallop the rider lifts his weight from the pony's back, moving his weight forward and gripping with his knees, so

In the children's pairs class the ponies show their paces under saddle. Here two smart greys perform together at the canter.

that he does not impede the animal's progress at this exacting pace.

The pony should be taught to perform well at all paces and to slow from the faster to the slower paces without any undue difficulty. Ponies can get very excited, especially in company, and it is not pleasant for a young rider to be run away with by an over exuberant mount. Schooling is very important for all ponies, especially young ones or those which are to be used for special purposes. Schooling merely consists of carefully formulated and performed sessions of lessons, with the pony either on the lungeing rein, ridden, or both. The lessons must never be boring for the pony and he must not become overtired or he will come to resent them. Only one major new lesson should be taught at any one session and when the pony has mastered it, he should be rewarded and put away in his stable or paddock to digest what he has learned. Then he can be tested on his learning ability the next day. Most ponies enjoy being schooled, and if properly fed and groomed so that they are in good health,

their performance can only be improved by these schooling periods.

Most ponies have a natural jumping ability, for in the wild, they would have to cross ditches, banks and other obstacles in their normal daily lives. Because of this they can be trained to develop this asset; most ponies really love jumping lessons. The first lessons are given from the ground, and the pony is merely led over poles which are laid flat on the ground. At this stage the pony is encouraged to step over the poles rather than jumping and must be kept calm and collected throughout the session. Before jumping lessons are given the pony must be thoroughly schooled and obedient at all other paces. It must be fit and supple and must use its hocks well.

Cavaletti are poles fixed to pairs of cross-shaped supports and made in such a way that they can be turned over to give small jumps of varying heights, usually 25cm, 35cm, and 45cm (9.8in, 13.7in, and 17.7in). The pony is schooled over the cavaletti first by leading, then by lungeing, and finally by being ridden. This

schooling teaches the pony to pick up his legs and to judge the distance over and between the poles, in fact it makes him think seriously about the job in hand. From the very beginning the pony must be taught to jump in style and to curve his back into a convex shape. A pony that jumps with its head up high and a straight back has to put much more energy into clearing an obstacle and will never be able to jump very high. It is likely that its hind-legs will come down on the jump. In schooling the pony to

jump, it must never be overfaced, that is, asked to take a jump too high for its capabilities. Ponies enjoy jumping as long as they are not frightened or hurt, and a height of 1m (3·28ft) is enough of an achievement in the early schooling sessions on the lunge. Having reached this stage, the pony goes back to the beginning again, this time carrying a rider and resumes the cavaletti sessions before attempting proper jumps. It is essential that the rider sits quietly and well forward and does not jab the pony's mouth while

jumping. It is often a good plan to put a strap around the pony's neck for the rider to hold while jumping to prevent this happening.

All jumping lessons, as indeed all schooling lessons, should be kept short and progressive as ponies can become quickly soured and lose interest if bored. Young ponies can suffer from strains if worked too hard while immature. As the pony becomes increasingly adept at jumping, the actual jumps should be modified and varied so that the animal will

Left
In the riding classes the conformation and action of the pony is assessed. Here the judge asks one young exhibitor to perform an individual, short display of her pony's paces.

Above
An immaculate turn-out, well deserving of the winner's ribbon. The young lady shows the correct way to ride side-saddle, and the pony is beautifully presented with well-fitting tack, plaited mane and tail and neatly water-brushed quarters.

jump any obstacle no matter how garish, narrow, or unusual, without balking or breaking his stride.

Well-proportioned, handsome ponies may make their mark in the riding classes of horse shows, but to be successful, they and their riders must be very well-schooled and fit, and both must be smartly turned out for the ring. In riding classes the conformation and paces of the pony are judged, and the expertise and bearing of the rider play a vital part. The rider's clothes must conform to certain standards and the pony must wear specific items of tack. Some types of bits and equipment are banned from certain classes and a thorough perusal of the rules is advised before embarking on a season of showing.

To be successful in the show-ring a pony must move well and be obedient, so normal schooling will have been carried out. The pony needs to have quality, so should be well-bred. If he trots out really well and points his toe, he will be sure to catch the judge's eye and the elusive quality known as 'presence' (the ability to exude charm) and a correct bearing also increases his chances. Before the show the pony must be made fit by proper exercise and feeding. The mane and tail must be pulled so that all unwanted hairs are plucked out well before the big

Right
This handsome liver-chestnut Welsh Cob is being held by his handler in the accepted position for the judge's inspection. He is wearing stallion tackle and is being exhibited in an in-hand class.

Far right
Foals are shown in-hand being led around the ring with their dam by means of a lead-rein attached to a well-fitting headcollar or foal-slip.

Below
The trot is an important pace for showing a pony's true action. Here a Welsh Cob trots out in-hand for the judges, moving freely and well for his young handler.

day, and all the long hairs on his chin and around his ankles are tidied up. The day before the show any white areas are carefully washed and dried, and the mane and tail are similarly treated if necessary. On the morning of the show the mane and tail are neatly plaited and properly sewn in with a long needle and button thread to match the hairs. After a thorough grooming, the pony has a tail-bandage applied, thick leg-bandages put on each leg and a light rug put over his back. His headcollar should be clean and safe and a stout rope with a good clip is attached.

Naturally the pony should have been taught to walk without fuss into a horse-box or trailer, and should lead in without any difficulty. If he does jib because of excitement, then some help may be required to encourage him up the ramp. A yard broom against his quarters will usually make him decide to load, or a long lunge rein around his quarters, held by two assistants can be used to ease him forward into the trailer. When he is loaded he should be rewarded and then tied up securely before setting off for the show. At the show ground the trailer should be parked in the shade if possible, and the pony unloaded. After grooming him thoroughly and oiling his hooves he can be tacked-up and given a warming-up ride around the show-ground.

When the class is announced, the pony and rider wait in the collecting ring, then the class enters the ring, usually in numerical order. The pony should be kept moving freely forward at all times and ridden well away from any other ponies who threaten to kick or otherwise misbehave. The judge's stewards instruct the riders when to walk, trot, canter or otherwise change pace or direction. It is important to ride the perimeter of the arena and not to cut the corners. The rider should talk to the pony and ride as well as possible. The judge will have the ponies called in to line up one by one. Then in some competitions the riders are asked to dismount and remove or strip the ponies of their saddles so that their conformation can be examined. When being examined the pony should be stood up so that his legs are all neatly arranged, one hind leg slightly behind the other. It is usual to lead the pony away from the judge, turn him around away from the rider, then trot him smartly back in a straight line to show off his straight action. Sometimes it is the custom to give a short ridden demonstration or 'show' for the judge, and the well-schooled pony and rider can perform neat circles and a figure-of-eight at the canter, changing diagonals in the centre with the movement known as the flying change. A controlled rein-back or turn can help to impress the judge with the pony's obedience.

As well as the ordinary show classes there are classes for less well-made ponies, which enable them to show other abilities such as being suitable as working or hunter ponies. In these classes the pony is called upon to perform simple manoeuvres, perhaps going through a latched gateway and jumping some low, unusual jumps. In some countries, special riding classes are held for ladies to show their ponies ridden side-saddle, and the skill of the rider using this seat is carefully assessed. Ponies of special types or breeds may also be shown in-hand, that is, led around the arena for assessment, instead of being ridden. These classes are

mainly for unbroken young stock, brood mares or stallions, but the condition, conformation and presentation of the pony is just as important as in the ridden classes. For in-hand showing the pony is led around the ring at the walk, then sometimes at the trot before the judge calls for it to join the line-up. Each pony is then examined and led out for inspection individually before the final judgment takes place.

Dressage is a word often surrounded with mystique, but it merely refers to the series of well-defined phases in the training of a pony which make it entirely obedient to the slightest aid given

by its rider. There are, of course, competitions in which certain dressage movements must be executed in order to accrue points, and in the competitions known as One-day or Three-day Events, each pony has to complete three events, a cross-country course, a show-jumping course and finally give a simple display of dressage movements. In dressage, the pony must move confidently and freely at all paces and the riders instructional aids must be quite imperceptible to the judge or audience. Even when at the halt, the pony must be alert and waiting for the next sign to be given by his rider.

Most ponies are capable of

For in-hand classes special bridles are used. They are made of good-quality leather and are designed to give a smart appearance as well as enabling the handler to control the pony.

learning a little dressage, and become better rides because the training makes them more responsive to their riders' requirements. In the **halt** the pony is taught to stand quite motionless and straight on all four legs, ready to move off in any direction upon command. The **ordinary walk** is free and quite unconstrained, the pony moving forward briskly with calm, even and resolute steps, the four-time beat regular and well-spaced. At the **extended walk** the pony strides out, but without undue haste, the head and neck stretched on an extended rein and the hind feet making tracks beyond those of the forefeet. The **free walk** is performed on a loose rein and gives the pony complete freedom of the head and neck during a brief rest period. In the **collected walk** the pony has his neck raised and arched with the head in an almost vertical position. The hind legs are brought well under the body and the pace, slower than the normal walk, is full of impulsion and style. In the **ordinary** and the **extended trot** the rider usually rises, while in the elegant **collected trot**, the sitting position helps to keep the pony moving in the characteristically slow, measured but energetic way. The **canter** is also executed at ordinary, extended and collected speeds, and many movements are incorporated as the pony moves around the arena in a dressage competition. He may be required to change direction several times or to perform the **change of legs** as we have previously described. All changes of pace or speed must be performed smoothly and without any conscious effort. After coming to a halt, the pony may be expected to **rein back**, which means that he must take an exact number of strides smoothly in reverse without swinging to the right or to the left. If he champs at his bit this will be construed as a wish to be obedient, but if he swishes his tail or grinds his teeth, the judges may mark him down. Other movements such as turns and passes can be taught to the well-schooled pony which is to be used for more advanced dressage work.

Whatever sort of showing the pony and rider undertake, the classes should be entered into seriously, but with good humour and a spirit of true sportsmanship. Not everyone can win and those who do not achieve a rosette or ribbon can always try again another day. The main object should be to ride as well as possible and to show the pony's paces at their very best. If a rosette is awarded, the judge should be thanked politely and the pony rewarded with a pat.

After showing, the pony should be relieved of his tack and rubbed down before being bandaged and rugged and loaded into the trailer for the journey home. After the journey he can be given a drink of water with the chill taken off before he is allowed his feed of corn, or a warm bran mash. His legs and feet must be thoroughly checked over for any signs of strains or swellings before he is left to have his well-earned rest.

There is, as we have seen, a class or event of some kind for every sort of pony whatever its shape, size or breeding. It is a good idea, if possible, to join a local Pony or Riding Club which can help in training and give advice on all aspects of pony management and equitation. Riding Clubs often have small and friendly shows for members in which they may gain experience, and Pony Clubs have local rallies at which visiting experts give talks and demonstrations of all kinds. Even those who do not own a pony can benefit from membership of Pony and Riding Clubs, many of which provide training schemes and examinations which measure progress in riding and stable management. Whether racing, jumping, hunting, trekking, driving, or merely hacking quietly along peaceful country roads, there is an aspect of the world of ponies to suit everyone, and an opportunity to develop that special working relationship that grows between a sympathetic rider and his regular mount.

Acknowledgements

Animal Graphics: 6, 13 bottom, 15, 16 top, 16 bottom, 17, 20, 21 top, 21 bottom, 32 top, 32 bottom, 33 top, 34, 35, 36, 44, 50, 51, 67 top, 67 bottom, 68, 69 top, 69 bottom, 71, 72, 73 top, 73 bottom, 74, 75, 76, 77, 78 top, 78 bottom, 79 top, 79 bottom, 80, 81, 82 top, 82 bottom, 83, 86, 87, 90, 91, 92 top, 92 bottom, 94, 95; *Ardea:* 7, I. R. Beames 37 top, Kevin Carlson 30, Jean-Paul Ferrero 70, Sue Gooders 26, P. Morris 29, C. K. Mylne 14; *Peter Baker:* 46 top; *Bruce Coleman Limited:* E. Breeze-Jones 31 bottom, Jane Burton 12, 18, Fritz Prenzet 37 bottom, Hans Reinhard endpapers; *Diederik D'Ailly, Toronto:* 22; *Equestrian (Press and General) Services Limited:* 84; *Paolo Koch:* 61 top, 61 bottom, 62 top; *Peter Roberts:* 11, 58, 89, 93; *Spectrum:* 42, 52, 53, 54, 64; *Tony Stone Associates:* 19, 23, 27, 59, 85; *Sally Anne Thompson:* 28, 31 top, 33 bottom, 38, 40–41, 48 bottom, 55 top, 55 bottom, 63, 66, 88; *John Topham Picture Library:* Topham/Windridge 56–57, Garard de Vecchio 24–25; *Nicholas Toyne:* 65; *Elisabeth Weiland:* 49 top, 49 bottom; *ZEFA:* D. Baglin 60, J. Bitsch 8–9, 10, K. E. Deckart 46, H. Helbing 39, Gerolf Kalt 45, 47, M. Linder 43, M. Pitner 62 bottom, Hans Reinhard 13 top, G. Rettinghaus title page.